The 50 Greatest Movies Never Made

Chris Gore

D0011896

 St. Martin's Griffin New York

Library of Congress Cataloging-in-Publication Data

Gore, Chris
    The 50 greatest movies never made / Chris Gore. — 1st St. Martin's
Griffin ed.
      p.   cm.
    ISBN 0-312-20082-X
    1. Unfinished motion pictures—United States.   2. Motion pictures—
United States Anecdotes. I. Title. II. Title: Fifty greatest movies
never made.
PN1995.G58   1999
791.43—dc21   99–24101
                                                      CIP

First St. Martin's Griffin Edition: July 1999

Design: James Sinclair

10 9 8 7 6 5 4 3 2 1

For Dennis Gore
Dad, you're the one who told me I should be a writer. Thanks.

Special Thanks

There are so many people to thank, here's a random list in no particular order of the people and organizations who, without their assistance, this book would not have been possible: my always supportive agent, Laurie Fox; my kick-ass editors, Jim Fitzgerald and Gordon Van Gelder; Rebecca Schuman; the most knowledgeable man alive when it comes to the craft of screenwriting, Jeff Gordon of the incredible Writer's Boot Camp; Sean Costello; Vicky Gallion; the Writers Guild of America; Jeb Brody; *Scenario Magazine;* Mark Altman; David E. Williams; Steven Pizello; *American Cinematographer* magazine; Jerry Beck; Arthur Borman; the Sundance Film Institute; Brad Schreiber; the American Film Institute; *Tease* magazine; Buddy Barnett; Cinema Collector's (a great store to visit if you are ever in Hollywood); *Cult Films* magazine; Greg Theakston; James Lorinz; Carol Lay; the readers of *Film Threat* magazine; Scott Alexander and Larry Karaszewski; Drew's Script-O-Rama; Mom (can't forget her); and especially my wife, Marion. I'd also like to thank all of the screenwriters, producers, directors, and filmmakers for their cooperation in this project. Don't ever give up. I thank you all sincerely.

CONTENTS

Introduction

If I'm reading your internal dialogue correctly, you think me presumptuous just to compile a list of the "greatest" almost-films. After all, who am I to determine which abortive projects are the "greatest" of all time? Movies are only movies when they become movies. An idea is not a movie; a screenplay is not a movie—even a bunch of unedited footage is not a movie. There's something magical about movies. They work in mysterious ways. Smart people in Hollywood are aware that no one really knows what makes a film good or bad.

Let me admit something to you. Frankly, I'm not exactly happy with the title of this book, *The 50 Greatest Movies Never Made.* It's only going to cause unnecessary debate, like any type of "greatest" list naturally does. Let me let you in on a secret—these are not really the "greatest." If I had my way, I'd rather title this book something like *The 50 Best, Coolest, Weirdest, Strangest, Wildest, Most Amazing, Most Fantastic, Most Stupendous, Most Remarkable, Most Incredible, Most Bizarre, and Potentially Greatest Movies That Never Happened.* But then again, try fitting all of that copy on the cover in a title visible from a distance of 10 feet. Obviously, it wouldn't work. I think marketing departments should do their job, and so the title is what it is. Live with it.

This book is about the world's greatest failures. Each of these films, made under the best of circumstances, had the potential to be one of the greatest, but we'll never know. In some cases, a script went through development, only to collect dust on some studio executive's shelf. In others, the film may have gotten very far along only to be prevented from completion by death, disease, or other tragic circumstances. And finally, some of these films actually began shooting only to be shut down by disaster or cold financial decision makers.

Each of the chapters you will read contain two twisted tales of Tinseltown:

1. The story of the film itself.
2. The story behind the story. Why did the film languish in development hell or get shut down or otherwise prevented from being born, kicking and screaming its way into movie theaters, where these movies belonged? Why?

Forty-two thousand screenplays written on spec are registered each year by the Writers Guild of America. Of those, approximately three thousand are bought, optioned, set up for development, and otherwise put into the Hollywood pipeline. Of those three thousand, fewer than fifty actually get made. Fewer than fifty! That means, statistically speaking, your chances of winning at those lottery scratchers games are better than your chances of selling a script. The odds are bad, but that doesn't stop Hollywood players or the dreamers from getting in the game.

Great directors fail, bad directors sometimes soar, and studio execs—don't even ask! Some of the best movies ever made have come from exceedingly bad ideas, and great ideas have borne the foulest of films. Ask any filmmaker about a recent failure, and he/she'll tell you, "The rushes looked great!" That's because a movie that's made is just what it is, but a movie that isn't made could have been anything.

There is an alternate universe of unfinished cinema, far larger than the library of films that we know. Some unfinished films are legendary; others are completely unknown. The same directors, writers, actors, and producers worked just as hard on their uncompleted films as on those that reached fruition. Since they weren't made, they will always be great—no one will muck them up.

When you read this book, your mind will see movies that might have been, that could have been. You will learn of the disappointments of great figures and the powers more powerful than the powerful. You will be in an alternate universe—a dimension very much like our own but for the fact that it never was. And no nitrate decomposition or color fading can ever rob you of what you've experienced between these covers. At the very least, you'll learn that even famous people don't always get what they want.

Many of these ideas were truly great. They might not have turned into great films, but as ideas they were truly great.

★ ★ ★

P.S. There are countless movie ideas that haven't made it to the screen—but only 50 of those are in this book, leaving plenty of room for a sequel. Which is very Hollywood thinking, if you ask me.

A Day at the UN

Do you think it would be funny to do a picture with the Marx Brothers at the United Nations?

Billy Wilder is widely regarded as one of the greatest film directors who ever lived. The Austrian-born, German-trained former newspaperman was a screenwriter before turning to directing. He is generally placed in the same pantheon as the great Preston Sturges, who inaugurated Hollywood's writer/director revolution of the 1940s.

The esteemed American critic Andrew Sarris, who popularized the French "auteur theory" in the United States, numbers Wilder among his favorite film authors. The auteur theory was conjured up by a collection of post–World War II French critics who held that some directors maintained recurring personal themes in their work and that these directors could be considered the authors of their films. Film is, of course, a collaborative medium, and the auteur theory does not assert that all directors are the authors of their films. As a matter of fact, the common misinterpretation that the theory proclaims the director is always the "auteur" of a film has resulted in a significant number of bad films during Hollywood's modern era. Nevertheless, Billy Wilder is truly an auteur, because he is quite literally the author of his films as their co-screenwriter and because they are fraught with recurring personal themes.

Wilder has made films in a variety of genres, and his output includes *Double Indemnity,* one of the definitive pieces of "film noir," as well as *Some Like It Hot,* the hilarious drag comedy. His oeuvre contains *The Lost Weekend* and *Witness for the Prosecution* as well as *Kiss Me, Stupid* and *The Major and the Minor.* By the 1960s, Wilder had turned almost exclusively to comedy, and in the post–*Some Like It Hot* era, the term *Billy Wilder film* pretty much suggested "comedy" to members of the audience. But this was a man who could summon despair as easily as hilarity.

Wilder's comic sense is, at least to some extent, an outgrowth of his fabled cynicism. And this cynical take on things causes even his

Director Billy Wilder might have made the greatest Marx Brothers film of all.

"serious" work to be laced with comedy. Even a bleak Wilder film like the alcoholism chronicle *The Lost Weekend* contains many comic moments. The classic *Sunset Boulevard* might even be called a black comedy. (In the film's original opening, the deceased William Holden was supposed to sit up in the morgue and tell the other corpses his tale.)

Sunset Boulevard of 1950, the tale of a washed-up silent star, is a perfect embodiment of one of the recurring motifs that define Wilder the auteur. The European who embraced America and became a primary creator of its motion pictures has had a fascination with and lifelong love of America's pictures and its stars—particularly from the era that first entranced him in his youth. *Sunset Boulevard,* of course, sees these enthusiasms through the prism of Wilder's cynicism. We are treated to a macabre look at what the once-grand figures of Hollywood's silent era had become. But soon thereafter, following a particularly dark Wilder effort called *Ace in the Hole,* the director decided to return to the theme from a much brighter perspective.

Wilder had observed that due to declining American box office during the early television era, the postwar European market was becoming responsible for an ever larger percentage of a motion picture's gross. He decided this meant that he could successfully make a feature starring Laurel and Hardy, despite their career eclipse in the States, since they were still popular overseas. He asked Norman Krasna to collaborate with him on the script, for which he had already contrived the basic story.

It would be set during Hollywood's silent era. The opening sequence would be a long shot of the Hollywood sign. Moving closer, we would discover two figures sleeping within the *O*s—Mr. Laurel and Mr. Hardy. They were to play movie extras who lived in a cemetery. A rich widow would meet Ollie while visiting her husband's grave and would fall in love with him, but she would hate Stanley! The classic "Who does Hardy love more?" situation would thus come into play.

Unfortunately, Krasna couldn't stand working with Wilder, who belittled him, and left the project. (He later helped Wilder with *Avanti!*) Wilder enlisted Edwin Blum to replace Krasna, whereupon Oliver Hardy up and got sick on them. Wilder ended up making *Stalag 17* instead. He returned repeatedly, however, to this period of American history and eventually returned to the notion of revisiting a classic comedy team.

While making 1960's *The Apartment* in New York City, Wilder was staying near the United Nations. He witnessed the cold war hubbub surrounding the place and one day asked his collaborator I. A. L. Diamond, "Do you think it would be funny to do a picture with the Marx Brothers at the United Nations?" Diamond took to the idea, and off they were to (a day at) the races.

Groucho liked the idea and told Wilder to make a deal with the group's agent, their brother Gummo. Gummo felt the deal was doable, so Wilder and Diamond developed the idea into a 40-page treatment.

Groucho was to be the leader of a mob that decides New York's police department is so tied up with UN delegate protection that it would be possible to rob Tiffany's unnoticed by the distracted officers. Chico was to be the "muscle" of the organization, Harpo its safecracker (shown in one scene to be unable to open even a can of sardines). Navigating the New York sewer system, they would steal four suitcases of diamonds from Tiffany's before attempting to escape on a tramp steamer bound for Brazil. There would, however, be an anti-Communist demonstration when they got to the pier, and somehow the police were to mistake them for the UN's Latvian delegation. They would be given a police escort to the Latvian embassy, just when they would otherwise have been able to escape. The comic climax was to have been a scene wherein Harpo addressed

The Marx Brothers were set to cause havoc at the United Nations. What a ride that would have been!

the entire General Assembly without uttering a sound—utilizing his classic bag of tricks, including horn honking and girl lunging, while multiple foreign interpreters "translated."

Unfortunately, as with Laurel and Hardy, age and infirmity crept in. Harpo had a heart attack while rehearsing for a TV special, and though his health improved, they were unable to get insurance for the project. Shortly thereafter Chico died, and that, of course, was that.

Wilder went on to do the Jimmy Cagney starrer *One, Two, Three,* which revisited the fast-talking style of some of Cagney's 1930s Warner Bros. movies.

It's a pity that we didn't get to see this potential Marx Brothers classic. Wilder was at his comic peak, having just made *Some Like It Hot* and *The Apartment* in rapid succession. Groucho was riding high, having starred for more than a decade in television's *You Bet Your Life*. Harpo's contemporaneous TV appearances indicate that he was undiminished by time. And this would have been only the Marxes' second chance to work with a top flight director. The first, their collaboration with Leo McCarey, had resulted in *Duck Soup,* perhaps their finest film.

The brothers had not worked much as a team during the previous decade or more but had recently warmed to the notion, having previously filmed a TV pilot called *Deputy Seraph.* Though there were no further Marx Brothers projects, Groucho did return to the greasepaint-mustached character in Otto Preminger's 1968 *Skidoo.*

Wilder later created his own classic comedy team by pairing Jack Lemmon and Walter Matthau in 1966's *The Fortune Cookie.* But neither Wilder nor the moviegoing audience got to enjoy the Marx Brothers by spending a day at the UN.

The Adventures of Fartman

Stern has said that "the deal fell through over Fartman coffee mugs."

There are two ways to dislike Howard Stern. One is by being a celebrity whose feelings are hurt by Stern's radio eruptions. The other is by never actually having heard him (only having heard about him).

Howard is not merely a "shock jock." Unlike the witless annoyances who compose the bulk of radio "comedy," Howard is not broadcasting primarily as an abrasive who rouses listeners from their slumber. He's there to be funny and to speak in the voice of the American proletariat. That voice is not always pretty, in the same way that rap music can be a drag. But if rap is the news of the ghetto, then Howard's rap is the rap of the common man.

The audience's connection with him has been borne out time and time again as his New York–based radio show has expanded to other markets. Stern, the outsider, tends to beat his local adversaries because being local doesn't mean his competitors have anything in common with their listeners. Howard speaks both to his audience and as his audience. He is one of them, even if from afar.

His audience has followed him from radio to books, from radio to television, and from radio to motion pictures. The move to motion pictures proved most fortuitous of all, for it demonstrated to many of Howard's critics what his audiences already knew: Howard is a real man, possessed of real feelings and real experiences. He is not just a venom-spewing machine. Viewed in that context, his volcanic verbalizations take on a different hue. It's one thing to read Howard's utterances in cold, black print. It's another to hear them directly, mitigated by the nature of the man.

This is not to argue that Howard's humor isn't coarse. His humor is coarse, of course (of course), but, equally important, it *is* humor. Howard's successful foray into video produced the classic *Butt-Bongo Fiesta* which could be considered a great experimental film.

Howard's screen debut in *Private Parts* (adapted from his book) won him many new fans and served to humanize him in the hearts and minds of the general public. There has been much less hue and cry over Howard since *Private Parts'* release. In its wake, he's been able to appear more mainstream, even crossing over into big-time television. Might a more authentic debut feature have offered not the man, but his work—the coarse, unvarnished voice of the people that radio fans have come to love and that critics hate?

It certainly was in Stern's character to do it that way. Early television efforts featured lesbian components and other inflammatory offerings. His first syndicated series even broadcast the adventures of a character called Fartman. The character had originated back when Stern was doing his radio show in Washington, D.C., and was a fine example of the unvarnished Howard.

Well, if things had gone according to plan, Howard would have made his movie debut with a character like that. In fact, he would have made his debut with that very character. *The Adventures of Fartman* was to have been Howard Stern's premiere theatrical release.

The visual appearance of Fartman, a superhero character, changed over the years leading up to his intended movie debut. On Stern's WWOR TV program, Fartman wore a toilet seat around his neck instead of the more traditional superhero cape. On 1992's MTV Music

Awards show, Fartman's outfit was glitzier. The character entered from above, and when he reached the stage a new costume innovation—exposed butt cheeks—was revealed. From between said cheeks (at least seemingly) came an explosion.

As you can see, by this point in the nineties both Howard's and Fartman's profiles were expanding. New Line Pictures decided that the time was right to bring Howard to the motion picture screen, and *Fartman* was believed to be a suitable vehicle.

Screenwriter Jonathan Lawton, who had written *Pretty Woman* and *Under Siege,* was brought on board to script the heroic opus. (Howard claimed that Lawton had seen him invoking Fartman on a Leno *Tonight* show and exclaimed, "That's my next picture!") A story was developed in which Howard was to play a New York editor who was also the powerful *Fartman!* His heroic counterpart was created when evildoers stuffed him with a sludgy compound that gave him "colonic powers."

The movie was thought capable of filling the *Wayne's World* niche and was expected to be a successful summer comedy. Unfortunately, though development did commence, Howard and New Line never actually came to terms regarding the picture. No contract was ever signed.

There was, however, a comic strip adaptation of the first five pages of the hilarious script. In the bowels of the city, we see a hooker getting roughed up by some ne'er-do-wells. Fartman, his face covered with stubble, arrives on the scene and blows the villains away (you know what I mean). The grateful hooker tells Fartman, "Any time you want a free one, just ask for Bruno."

The hooker turns out to have been a transvestite, and a disappointed /disgusted Fartman "turns the other cheek and is gone with the wind."

Stern has said that "the deal fell through over Fartman coffee mugs." In truth, New Line, which had missed out on a fortune because they didn't have the licensing rights to the characters in their

Teenage Mutant Ninja Turtles movies, didn't want to make the same mistake again. The 5 percent licensing interest reportedly offered to Howard just wasn't sufficient as far as the comedian was concerned.

Also, Howard had envisioned *Fartman* as an R-rated movie, while the studio apparently wanted it to be PG-13—yet another bone of contention.

It may have been a better career move for Howard to have made *Private Parts*, but fans were deprived of the opportunity to get their comic savagery undiluted. It's very possible that more people would have gone to see *Fartman* than attended *Private Parts*. But *Fartman* would never have humanized Howard in the minds of the media the way *Private Parts* did. The world, however, has enough humans. There was only one Fartman.

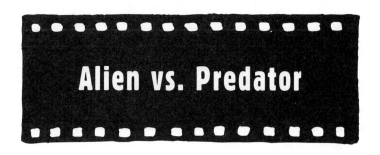

Alien vs. Predator

Ext. Deep Space
We OPEN on TOTAL BLACKNESS, a sea of stars
spread across the infinite depths of space. As the
TITLES ROLL, we notice that three of these specks
seem to be moving; one of them picking up
acceleration and racing toward us. Our perspective
changes, and we catch a quick glimpse as it
HURTLES past, and into the gravitational pull of a
large brownish planet. Kicking up SPARKS of
FRICTION as it hits atmosphere. It seems to be
manmade. Or at least artificial.

The preceding was the beginning of a spec screenplay, which is a film script that has been written with the hope that it will sell. The speculation is on the part of the writer that when he finishes his script a producer will whip out a checkbook and buy it. That speculation is almost always wrong. The fragment that opened this chapter was, as a matter of fact, the opening of a particularly difficult kind of spec script—a spec script based on existing material that someone else already owns.

Now, let me explain that though a spec script is unlikely to sell, there are still good reasons for writing one. They serve as writing samples and can help get you an agent or even a job. And when they're particularly suited to the marketplace they can be sold for a good deal more money than one earns when writing under studio assignment.

As a result, even big-time writers do spec scripts, because it gives them the opportunity to lay down precisely what the movie will be about before the studio gets to tamper with it (which they will do in any event) and to get more money than if they were writers for hire. If you're attempting to break into the sitcom-writing game, you *must* have a couple of spec scripts based on this month's hottest shows. Moreover, you must expect your agent will not even attempt to sell them to the shows for which they were written. They will serve as samples of what you can do and help you get a staff job on something bad.

But this scenario only works in television. In the movie world, there is never any reason to write a spec script based on somebody else's product. Only fanboys do this; often those with a *Star Trek, Star Wars,* or James Bond fixation. If you do this, people in Hollywood will be scared of you and you will be laughed at and avoided by all. Yet that's what the fanboy who wrote the script segment at the opening of this chapter did. He wrote a spec script based on the Dark Horse comic *Alien vs. Predator.*

And he sold it to 20th Century-Fox.

Peter Briggs, the writer in question, explained the circumstances to a reporter: "I looked around and the very first *Alien vs. Predator* comic was just about to come out, and I thought—'That's it.' And I wrote it. I finished it, I think, just as the last comic came out. The comic's great, you can't fault it. Dark Horse, to their credit, thought about putting it together, and I'm a big fan of Phil Norwood's art, who did the original artwork—great guy, great storyboard artist, the guy's a hero in the field."

Briggs continued, "What I did was take the bare frame of the story, eject everything from it that didn't work, and put in a whole lot more material. So I think probably there's about 70–75% of me in there."

His representatives reacted appropriately.

"When I handed it in to my agent, he looked horrified, because he had no idea I was writing it, and assumed rightly it'd be a tough sell. He said, 'Well, I've got to go across to LA next week,' . . . and so he took it in to Larry Gordon . . . who had been asked the week before by Fox to come up with this! And bang, we were away."

Great story, huh? Briggs got to revise his draft and everything. He got paid—that's a big deal. It's like a Cinderella story.

Except the movie never got made.

Still, there were bonuses. Briggs was considered for other interesting writing jobs. For instance, he was one of several writers hired to write a script for a different franchise combination, the *Friday the 13th/Nightmare on Elm Street* merger titled *Freddy vs. Jason* (among other things). Eventually, the studio decided to commission a new script by another writer and several scripts, including Briggs's were left in the dust.

Some business.

And it's actually rather odd that having come this far, some version of *Alien vs. Predator* didn't get made. The concept of pitting the sci-fi hunter characters of *Predator* against the unstoppable killers of the *Alien* movies has shown great commercial viability via comics, video games, and other marketplace indicators.

Int. Predator Mothership—Viewing Gallery
The gallery seems to be more mechanical than the rest of the ship. BROKEN TUSK enters, pausing next to a kind of readout device: a cylindrical tube containing a substance similar to mercury which

constantly changes its mass into shapes and alien text. He peers over the protective railing.

WHAT HE SEES is magnificent: a captive QUEEN ALIEN, the nucleus of the ALIEN society, fed by giant intravenous pipes. Each of its limbs is tethered by restraining clamps preventing any movement. To the rear, its giant egg-sac glows and throbs, suspended by a jury-rigged sling. A SCANNING MECHANISM hangs above the EGGS the QUEEN lays, seemingly defying gravity. As each EGG is scanned by a blue triangular beam—similar to a PREDATOR gunsight—it becomes translucent, giving us a view of the pulsing FACEHUGGER inside. This done, a manipulator carefully loads several eggs onto a pallet, which then sinks into a hatchway in the floor. It's an assembly-line of almost frightening mechanical efficiency.

You can see what's going to happen. Cool big-screen fighting between alien races. That's what this kind of movie is all about. This is a quintessential combination. Anybody who's read the script knows this film would have been awesome, pumping new life into Fox's *Alien* franchise.

But maybe that's the problem. Plenty of people have read the script.

Briggs told *Fusion* magazine, "Part of the problem is that now the first draft is so well-known. I don't know where it first leaked; I was only aware of it when somebody told me they'd seen it at a science fiction convention in LA. I guess it must have snuck out of a reader's office. Power of the photocopier. I found a copy in German the other day—someone had translated it into German. So part of the problem is that so many people know the story so well . . . but if you've got a story called *Alien vs. Predator*, you pretty much know what's going to happen, right?"

Right, Peter. But if you write a spec script based on somebody else's material, you already know what's going to happen, too. You're not going to sell it. So, you've already defied the odds to an unparalleled degree. Congratulations, Peter. You did what every genre fan dreams of. You took the bull by the horns and tried to get something you knew was right done the right way.

And you almost did it. That's amazing.

An American Tragedy

The story of a bright young man caught in the demands of straitlaced Protestant society, who eventually kills the girl he's made pregnant, was suited to Eisenstein's outlook.

Sergei Eisenstein was not simply one of the greatest directors in the history of film; he was also a significant figure in the development of film's language. Belonging to the Russian school of cinema, which believed that films were made in the editing, Eisenstein proved with *Potemkin* (1925) and *October* (1927) that his method of montage might not be the only way to make a movie, but it sure was a great way to go.

As with other top European directors, Hollywood came a knock, knock, knockin' on Eisenstein's door. The director was chatted up regarding American projects such as *Grand Hotel* and *The Life of Zola* and ultimately signed with Paramount. There were differences, however, between Eisenstein's situation and that of other European talents in Hollywood, because in 1930 Russia was little more than a decade into the Communist era.

Eisenstein had come up in the Communist universe. He was a believer of sorts, and his filmmaking triumphs were works of propaganda as well as art. While all films are a kind of propaganda, Hollywood's was the propaganda of Mom and apple pie (and all the good and the bad that goes with them). Russian films, on the other hand, were designed to support and sustain "the revolution." Within a short time, Hollywood would be full of Germans fleeing from the Nazis, who would make a significant contribution to American film. Eisenstein, however, was fleeing from nothing. He didn't see himself as a refugee from Soviet oppression. Russia was his home. He was in America just to make some art.

With the coming of sound, Eisenstein was interested in expanding his mastery of the visual into a new kind of audiovisual montage. He was excited about the possibilities of playing with sound as he had played with image. He wanted "a symphony of music, laughter and the natural sounds." Eisenstein enthused over the notion of ultralarge screens upon which pictures could be projected, just as some Americans did. But he went further. At one point he promoted the notion of a "dynamic square" for motion pictures, whereby the shape and size of the projected image would change as required. This is not the kind of thinking Hollywood wanted its directors to waste time with—especially not if they were serious.

While still in Russia, Eisenstein had conjured the idea for a film to be called *The Glass House*. It would center around a transparent apartment building in an American city. At first, people would go about their business as usual, and as long as their focus remained private everything would be all right. Over time, however, they would begin to move beyond their established propriety. They would start to notice things. They would see the way their neighbors lived. They would see suicide; they would see arson. Eventually, their lives would be about "watching." The walls and ceilings would seem to be made of faces. Eisenstein would present cold voyeurism in a montage of images and sounds. This was the first project he presented to his new bosses in America.

They wanted a "plot."

Eventually, it was decided that Eisenstein would write and direct a film version of the novel *An American Tragedy*. Such luminaries as

Griffith and Lubitsch had previously attempted to transfer Theodore Dreiser's tale to the screen, but without success. Eisenstein jumped at the challenge, seeing in the saga elements that connected with him as an artist.

The story of a bright young man caught in the demands of strait-laced Protestant society, who eventually kills the girl he's made pregnant, was suited to Eisenstein's outlook. He was quoted as being "interested at that time in films about society's mores, which affected Clyde in everything he did: the ruckus of election fever and his work for the re-election of the governor which broke him."

In his memoirs, Eisenstein described his take on the underlying elements of the story's structure:

I was deeply struck by the role of fate in Dreiser's An American Tragedy. *In my "treatment" of it for Paramount, I emphasized this tendency in every possible way. Clyde arranged Roberta's murder perfectly. Then came the notorious "change of heart": his change of plans when he was in the boat. And subsequently, the genuinely disastrous occurrence of Roberta's death. Once the implacable cogs were set in motion, the machine of crime turned everything Clyde had undertaken in his plan for committing the murder into the chain of evidence against him.*

Eisenstein continued: "Once set in motion, the fatal machine of crime followed its path automatically, like it or not, whether or not he oppose it, or try to escape its criminal intent (once it had been set in motion)." He compared this "image of implacable, automatic, mechanical progress" with the "impersonal, faceless (no close-ups!) column of soldiers" that had moved down the Odessa steps in his classic *October*.

Eisenstein felt his version of *An American Tragedy* was aborted because of "the risk of political scandal." He wrote: "The novel was banned for insulting common decency: Clyde and Roberta's adulterous affair, attempted abortions (and latent propaganda in favor of abortion), and the ensuing murder . . ." He wrote that the Paramount brass had "aspired to make this 'scandalous' novel a run-of-the-mill . . . tale of 'boy meets girl.' "

And it's true that Paramount went on to make a bland, compromised version of the story under the direction of Josef von Sternberg. Eisenstein reported that he was unable to sit through von Sternberg's version. And Theodore Dreiser sued Paramount over its handling of the material.

Paramount executive David O. Selznick had appreciated the artistry of Eisenstein's adaptation but believed the Eisenstein version could not "possibly offer anything but a most miserable two hours to millions of happy-minded young Americans." Eisenstein's propaganda—an indictment of America's social structure—was directly at odds with Hollywood's propaganda: the glorification of America's social structure.

Some twenty years later, a number of American filmmakers who had been idealistic communists during the 1930s were pilloried for allegedly putting communist precepts into Hollywood films. This couldn't be done, by them or by Sergei Eisenstein. Eisenstein wasn't allowed to tell an uncompromised American tale.

Before returning to Russia, Eisenstein got involved in another North American misadventure, titled *Que Viva Mexico*. He was bankrolled by muckraking American journalist Upton Sinclair and shot forty hours of footage (including multiple takes) before returning to Russia. He returned because of a telegram to Sinclair from Joseph Stalin. The telegram said that back in Russia Eisenstein was "THOUGHT TO BE A DESERTER WHO BROKE OFF WITH HIS OWN COUNTRY."

Eisenstein returned to Russia, and Sinclair promised the footage would be sent to him there. Sinclair, considered something of a communist here in America, never sent the footage.

Yet to come for Eisenstein would be the triumph of *Ivan the Ter-*

rible, Part One and the disappointments of the incomplete parts 2 and 3. He was both damned and praised at home and abroad. He died at the age of 50, in February of 1948. He will not be forgotten.

And neither will his treatment by the American film industry, which was, if you'll pardon the expression, an American tragedy.

A Trip To Mars

We have found that the theater-going public likes the unreal, the weird, and the uncanny . . .

U niversal Pictures during the 1930s was a veritable house of horror. *Dracula, Frankenstein, The Invisible Man, The Mummy* . . . a cycle of horror was created there that helps define the studio to the present day. The cycle was foisted upon Universal Pictures founder Carl Laemmle and his advisers by the studio's head of production, Carl Laemmle Jr. (How'd he get that job?) Nepotism aside, Junior turned out to be an exceptional film producer, and he pursued his passions, including the horror films, despite the objections of the older Universal hands.

James Whale, director of the classic *Bride of Frankenstein*, would never see his planned epic, *A Trip to Mars*, produced.

Universal's older management seemed mired in more established notions of what subjects were likely to make popular films. Laemmle Sr., for example, is quoted as saying, "I can't understand why we don't make dog pictures. Dog pictures always make money." Regardless, Laemmle Jr. showed that he was right in his assessment of the public taste, and posterity is the better for it.

One exceptionally compelling fantasy begun by the Laemmle Jr. regime in 1932 was *A Trip to Mars,* from a 27-page story by then-staffer Henry O. Hoyt. Hoyt had been a director for First National Pictures during the silent era and had worked on the famous dinosaur epic *The Lost World,* which featured Willis O'Brien's amazing stop-motion animation. *A Trip to Mars* was planned as a combination of live action and stop-motion about "strange half-mechanical creatures" at war with "giant insects with almost human intelligence." There were a number of treatments written and at least one screenplay before the project was taken off the front burner in favor of other Universal ideas.

Meanwhile, of all the men who had moved forward Carl Laemmle Jr.'s vision for his father's company, none had succeeded with as much impact and panache as James Whale. Whale, the director of *Frankenstein, The Old Dark House,* and *The Invisible Man,* among other efforts, was a supreme directorial stylist, hailed even in his own time as one of the masters of the screen. He had more than delivered the goods via his contributions to Junior's fantastic films cycle and was champing at the bit to try other story forms. Unfortunately, the success of his more gothic efforts doomed Whale to suffering the studio's insistence that he deliver more films in that vein. On the other hand, his success also gave him the leverage to demand some concessions from his studio masters.

An arrangement was worked out whereby Whale could direct one film from a different genre for every horror/fantasy picture he would direct. From Whale's perspective, this ensured that he would have the opportunity to direct a variety of stories that might catch his directorial fancy. From the studio's point of view, this meant they would be assured of a continuous stream of Whale fantasy classics to satisfy audiences and bean-counting shareholders as before.

The Invisible Man, Whale's most recent classic, had been so successful that the studio set up a department devoted to trick photography, such as was employed to great effect in that flick. It was understood that Whale's next fantasy epic would be either a *Frankenstein* sequel or *A Trip to Mars*.

In the wake of the recent RKO hit *King Kong* (with definitive stop-motion work by Willis O'Brien) and Whale's own "trick" effort, *The Invisible Man, A Trip to Mars* had been revived. Whale and his frequent collaborator R. C. Sherriff began work on *Mars* in October of 1933, and the script was nearly completed by December 19. Whale added humor to the picture by making the scientist, Professor Saxmor, less insane. He also added a henpecked millionaire who finances Saxmor's mission in order to get away from his wife.

The script also featured the professor's Irish terrier, who would learn to talk on Mars and would die in an attack of giant ants, uttering a final funny quip. Whale said the film would "soar higher into the realms of trick photography than *The Invisible Man*."

Whale went abroad for two months, and when he returned to Hollywood, Universal had suddenly changed. Laemmle Jr. was no longer in charge of production; the old guard had prevailed. Eventually, Laemmle Sr.'s son-in-law was put in charge of production, merely a lateral nepotistic step. Laemmle Jr. actually talked of retiring, even though he was only 26. (He did retire by the age of 29.)

Nevertheless, work on Whale's pictures continued. There was feeling at the studio that *A Trip to Mars* was a likelier follow-up to *The Invisible Man* than what was then being called *The Return of Frankenstein*. They found, however, that the stop-motion effects for *Mars* would take so long to prepare that they let Whale make a nonfantasy film first, while the *Mars* effects were prepared.

Unfortunately, time and management changes caused the project to lose momentum. While on April 30, 1934, *Daily Variety* had reported that James Whale's next picture was to be *A Trip to Mars*, by September Universal was simply saying it was "highly possible."

Whale made *The Bride of Frankenstein* instead. Produced by Junior Laemmle, it was a smash, and Junior was reinstated as head of production.

By this time, Whale was big enough to do whatever he wanted. He directed an adaptation of the Broadway musical *Show Boat* that is still regarded as one of the best stage-to-film musical translations ever made. But soon the Laemmles would be out of Universal forever, Whale would retire in frustration from the screen, and *A Trip to Mars* would remain unmade.

Stop-motion animation, trick photography, a 1930s-era Martian milieu, Universal fantasy production values, the humor and style of the great James Whale—it's a tragedy this film was never produced. Some believe that the success of *Flash Gordon* as a serial put the final nail in the coffin of this space fantasy feature.

Carl Laemmle Jr. once said, "We have found that the theater-going public likes the unreal, the weird, and the uncanny . . ."

Amen.

The Betty Page Story

Sexy but sweet. Betty chose her own life in a time when it wasn't allowed, she never had a manager, got to the top of her craft without walking on anybody's back.

Betty Page was a model and actress who appeared in nude stills and movies during the era that came between World War II and the Sexual Revolution. Unlike many of her contemporaries, Betty possessed a "girl next door" freshness that belied the theoretically sordid nature of her trade. She seemed the voluptuous embodiment of wholesome, all-American sex appeal and appeared in a variety of short films and photos until the early 1960s. Then she vanished, presumably to be forgotten forever.

Though obscure for many years, Page has gradually become relatively well-known. The fifties-era pinup queen fires imaginations today, just as she did during her youthful heyday, but now there's an added factor—the mystery of Betty herself. Why did this very public creature vanish so thoroughly? Where did she go? What did she do?

In recent years, books have come out that purported to answer these questions and several screen treatments of her life have been developed. There is no doubt that the story of the rise and retreat of Betty Page would make a truly satisfying cinematic experience. And

The Queen of Curves, Betty Page has had no less than four screenplays written about her tumultuous life, yet none of them has made it to the screen.

one of the several parties who attempted to develop a Betty Page feature was writer/artist/publisher Greg Theakston, who, on the basis of passion alone, conjured a project of extraordinary merit. Theakston had admired Page via sneak peeks at the dirty books of his youth and was one of the two men most responsible for the renewal of interest in her.

The other important Page venerator was comic book artist Dave Stevens. His *Rocketeer* featured a character named Bettie that was directly modeled on Miss Page. Stevens's new renderings of her image, combined with Theakston's reprintings of her photographs in his magazine aptly titled the *Betty Pages*, were primarily responsible for the Page revival.

Theakston's and Stevens's work eventually caused Page to resurface. Though she hasn't made any official public appearances, she has made her continued existence known. Theakston has had the opportunity to remunerate her for his reprintings of her work, while Page and Stevens have become friendly and have even gone to the movies together.

Theakston's enthusiasm for Betty began when he was a kid and received a call from a friend:

There was a strange urgency in his voice. "Get over here right away! I've found something!" I hung up and bolted across the yard without even putting a jacket on. He ushered me through the house and into his father's music study, and knelt in front of the blond-wood bookcase. I knelt, too. He pointed to the bottom drawer of a set that had been built into the bookcase. "This is the drawer that must never be opened," he proclaimed, and with a dramatic gesture, he pulled on the handle. My eyes popped out of my head as a stack of skin-magazines a foot deep came into view.

Theakston continued:

Murph's dad had very good taste when it came to girlie books. He had a selection of everything from Playboy *to nudist magazines, and a smattering of men's magazines that had been published over the preceding five years. Murph wouldn't allow me to touch them, and I was satisfied to let him turn the pages. We were careful not to get them out of order, for fear of discovery. . . . Inside some of the cheaper magazines we found women who were scary, decked out in strange outfits, sporting heavy make-up and weird hairstyles. That's the first time I ever saw a picture of Betty Page, top pin-up queen of all time.*

From that day in 1962 into the modern era, Theakston has carried a torch for Betty Page. And he used that torch to ignite a forest fire of interest in her when he began the *Betty Pages.* Soon thereafter, so many producers called Theakston asking if he knew of scripts based on her life that he decided to write one on his own.

Says Theakston:

I'd been researching her life and probably knew more about her than any writer in the world. I've been doing comic books and sto-ryboard art for twenty-five years, so writing my first script wasn't as hard as I thought it would be. . . . It was a great story waiting to be told. A woman's picture for sure, but lots to entertain the men. Sexy but sweet. Betty chose her own life in a time when it wasn't allowed, she never had a manager, got to the top of her craft without walking on anybody's back. A definite role-model for modern women.

He elaborated:

It's the story of Betty's time in New York City, 1950–57, the Eisenhower era. It's the story of a woman who resists what the world expects her to be and wins because of it, with a liberal dose of lingerie and cheesecake. Individuality triumphs in a world of taboo sexuality, until the Senate Sub-Committee investigation into pornography. Then Betty becomes a martyr for human sexuality.

Casting the part of Betty would be the key to the success of any project based on the life of the pinup queen. Kim Catrall once developed a rival Betty project with the intention of playing the lead, yet her project went nowhere. Theakston seriously considered Janine Turner of *Northern Exposure* fame, but this author believes that Christina Ricci, in the couple of years it'll take to get the picture made, would provide the ideal mixture of wholesomeness and intense sexuality. Thus far, of course, despite all the interest in Theakston's work, the Page picture has still not been made.

Theakston believes the picture's period setting makes it a little too expensive for producers to leap at, especially considering that it's not an effects-driven blockbuster. He also acknowledges that the Betty cult is still relatively small. He says lots of producers don't understand the power of her persona: "She's an icon, like Madonna."

Recent reports on Page have concentrated for the first time on her whereabouts during the "missing years"—her problems with alcohol, her legal problems (one book includes a mug shot), her "born-again" status. All of these things are interesting, but *Ed Wood* turned out to be a magnificent picture without focusing on Wood's years of decline.

One thing's for certain—as Greg Theakston continues to fan the flame of Page's greatness, interest will undoubtedly continue to grow.

Biker Heaven

Biker Heaven was to be a violent black comedy about the destruction of the American Dream.

Sometimes a movie can speak for a generation. When that happens, all the people involved in the picture are thought of as standard-bearers for that generation. *Easy Rider* (1969) was the spark for the entire seventies revolution in Hollywood moviemaking. Dennis Hopper, Jack Nicholson, Peter Fonda, Bob Rafelson—these names conjure up a moment in time, a lifestyle, a specific world both on and off the screen.

Peter Fonda was prepared for a trip to *Biker Heaven*, the planned sequel to *Easy Rider*.

Yet these people had been around for a long time before *Easy Rider*, and if that credit were removed from their résumés they would represent neither a generation nor a movement. At best, for example, Fonda might represent the biker genre in the way that Gabby Hayes is representative of B Westerns.

For God's sake, Dennis Hopper had been in movies in the fifties! Jack Nicholson had been a Hollywood actor since the fifties and had started his career in '53 or so at the MGM cartoon studio, working for the likes of Tex Avery, Bill Hanna, and Joe Barbera.

Peter Fonda was the son of Hollywood royalty and had made a name for himself in Roger Corman movies like *The Wild Angels.* Producers Bert Schneider and Bob Rafelson had been most successful with the Monkees—widely criticized as an imitation of the Beatles designed to represent youth culture of the day.

As a matter of fact, Bert Schneider was the son of Abe Schneider, who ran Columbia Pictures, and no more a Hollywood outsider than Peter Fonda. And if *Easy Rider* had been made as originally intended, it would have been seen as just another biker film—perhaps a particularly good one, but no more than another anarchic feather in the cap of producer Corman.

You see, Fonda and Hopper were originally going to make *Easy Rider* for Corman. The shift to Rafelson and Schneider (and their partner Steve Blaustein) might have made all the difference to the film's prospects. For one thing, the film's new producers *wanted* to be at the forefront of a new era in film. (They had previously dismantled their Monkees in the deconstructionist epic *Head,* written by Jack Nicholson.) For another, the film would now be distributed by Columbia Pictures. None of these things individually guaranteed that the film would rock the industry—in fact, no one could have predicted that—but each element, as it fell into place, provided a foundation for the "quintessence" that would come.

Easy Rider did become a monumental success. Hopper and Fonda entered a kind of permanent hippiedom in the public mind. Rafelson and Schneider went on to become the "padrones" of the new era, despite the fact that both were already over thirty. Rafelson directed *Five Easy Pieces,* among other important films. Nicholson, after more than a decade of obscurity, became one of the biggest stars in the history of film.

The road picture about a couple of bikers traveling across America touched a nerve and legitimately represented its moment. But as we have seen, such perfection is usually as much the result of accident as intent. That's one of the reasons sequels rarely have the impact of their predecessors. The original film was contrived spontaneously; the sequel is merely contrived—a methodical effort to replicate the tone and success of the original. Hell, in the modern era sequels are often little more than remakes. They don't continue the story; they repeat it! But—perhaps appropriately—the intended sequel to *Easy Rider* was an exception.

Dennis Hopper and Peter Fonda blaze trails from the classic *Easy Rider*. The duo planned to return for a tripped-out sequel called *Biker Heaven*.

Biker Heaven—the projected sequel—was blessed from the outset with certain circumstances that set it apart from the rest of the sequel pack. For one thing, its two lead characters had been killed at the end of the first picture! Yes, I know, the death of Spock and all that, but this was not science fiction and we were dealing with the equivalent of the deaths of Kirk *and* Spock!

Another blessing was that producer Bert Schneider was the kind of guy who really wanted to do great things. He wasn't a typical entrant in the sequel business.

And finally, the film was blessed by the fact that its makers recognized that time had passed since the era of the original film. And the 13 years that had elapsed between *Easy Rider*'s release in 1969 and *Biker Heaven*'s construction in 1982 were a *big* 13 years. (The 17 years from then to now were not as time-altering.) The hippie era had given way to the disco era, which had given way to the Reagan era. Acid rock had been supplanted by corporate rock, which had become less popular than disco, which gave way to punk turned new wave. And the writers of *Biker Heaven* knew this, for *Easy Rider*'s makers had seen fit to entrust the continuation of their creation to a writer who had lived through all the changes but was very much a representative of the present—Michael O'Donahue, fresh from the recently groundbreaking *Saturday Night Live*. (O'Donahue was himself an example of the sorts of accidents that can make or break a moment. If *Saturday Matinee,* his collaboration with Chevy Chase, had been made a few years earlier, we might have seen an entirely different movement in cinematic comedy. On the other hand, even if it had been made, but with him as the director—which was not likely to have been the case—it might have turned out as "memorably" as *Mr. Mike's Mondo Video.*)

The choice of O'Donahue as writer of an *Easy Rider* sequel was not as odd as it may seem, since O'Donahue had recently been collaborating at *Saturday Night Live* with Terry Southern, who was a credited coauthor of the original. And O'Donahue's presence assured that this would be a film of and for the eighties. (Some of the *Easy Rider* principals now say that Southern did no real writing on the original. If so, his involvement with the sequel was in the spirit of the original, because he was again credited as coauthor though he apparently contributed only a few lines.)

Biker Heaven was to be a violent black comedy about the destruction of the American Dream. It was set in the year 2068 (get it?), after a nuclear apocalypse. Billy and Captain America are brought back to life and sent by the Biker God to recover the revolutionary "Don't Tread on Me" American flag. Their mission: to bring about a rebirth of America.

They snort Chief Crazy Horse's granulated skull and travel across post-Armageddon America encountering the tribes that now inhabit it. Among those they meet are the Aryan Krusaders, the Cycle Sluts, the Black Panzers, and the Desert Demons. (My favorites are the Cannibal Cops.) Eventually, they make it to what had been our nation's capital and use the flag to (metaphorically) flog those who crushed the American dream. Americia's rebirth can now begin, so as a hard rock rendition of "The Battle Hymn of the Republic" plays, our two heroes burst into flames and travel back home to *Biker Heaven*. This is great work. O'Donahue and his collaborators Nelson Lyon and Terry Southern (sort of) had crafted a picture that was of the now but that did not do a disservice to the then. Unfortunately, not all of the necessary accidents were in place to make this moment happen.

Producer Bert Schneider was not as powerful as he had once been. Peter Fonda was not a bankable star at the time. Michael O'Donahue was not a factor in the movie business. Dennis Hopper had not yet returned from the abyss.

Biker Heaven was consigned to Unmade Movie Script Heaven.

And now Terry Southern and Michael O'Donahue are in real Heaven (we hope!). But Peter Fonda was nominated for an Oscar for *Ulee's Gold*. And Dennis Hopper is a bona fide star.

So, maybe someday, someone will finally make *Biker Heaven*. But for now, it remains one of the greatest films never made.

The Blind Man

The list of projects developed to one degree or another by Hitchcock is as enticing in its way as the list of films Hitch actually made.

Alfred Hitchcock had a meticulous way of filmmaking that led people to say his movies were completed before he even filmed them. Generally, his films were painstakingly storyboarded, shot by shot, so that no element was left to chance. A Hitchcock film's uncommonly taut precision is likely the result of this detail-intensive labor. And when you work in this fashion, you're likely to have a number of projects that get developed pretty far before they are eventually left incomplete.

The list of projects developed to one degree or another by Hitchcock is as enticing in its way as the list of films Hitch actually made.

Village of the Stars was a story about a plane that is given an order to drop an atomic bomb, only to have the order rescinded. Unfortunately, the bomb has been let partially loose from its compartment, and so the dilemma is that it has to be dropped somewhere!

The Short Night was a spy thriller to have taken place (at least in part) at the Russian/Finnish border.

A project called *Frenzy* (different from the later film and also called *Kaleidoscope*) was to have been about a misshapen psychopath murderer who is the son of a respected general and a homosexual. (Universal, at the time, was not surprisingly appalled.)

Hitchcock harbored a decades-long desire to adapt James Barrie's *Mary Rose* for the screen and was planning on making it his follow-up to *Marnie* when he had a falling out with intended star Tippi Hedren.

Hitch also talked about making *The Wreck of the Mary Deare* and *Trap for a Solitary Man,* which would have been based on a French play.

And one notable Hitchcock film that very nearly got made was titled *No Bail for the Judge.* The film was to be released by Paramount

Director Alfred Hitchcock was set to reach new heights in suspense with *The Blind Man.* Unfortunately, the film was never to be.

and was to star Audrey Hepburn, John "the Other Mr. French" Williams, and Laurence Harvey. It was adapted by Samuel Taylor from a novel by a British judge named Henry Cecil Leon. Hitchcock and Taylor worked out the visual story completely before even beginning work on the dialogue.

John Williams was to have been a judge who, while trying to help a dog, trips and falls on his head in the street. He manages to get up but—seemingly drunk—is taken by a prostitute to her home. He falls asleep and when he wakes up she is lying dead on the bed with a knife in her back! Remembering nothing, the judge figures he must have done it and calls the police.

Audrey Hepburn was to have played the judge's daughter, a British trial attorney who doesn't believe her father can be guilty of the crime.

And Laurence Harvey would have played a classy thief who agrees to help Hepburn (in exchange for not being arrested) into the criminal realm in order to exonerate her pa.

Hitchcock being so meticulous, Paramount was even prevailed upon to secure the services of an ex-hooker for Samuel Taylor to interview in an attempt to gain insight and detail into the netherworld. (Hitch wasn't at the interview, but he subsequently wanted to hear every bit of the ex-hooker's story.)

At a certain point in the development of the piece, Hitchcock handed the notes he had been accumulating over to Paramount, whereupon an executive asked just what that pile of paper was. Hitch replied, "These pieces of paper are in the process of becoming what you will one day refer to as 'our picture.'" That day, however, was not destined to come because Audrey Hepburn refused to do the picture, objecting to a scene in which her character was to be dragged into Hyde Park and raped.

It's probably a good thing that this picture was abandoned, because it seems like a potentially uncomfortable mix of old Hitchcock and new. He had just made *North by Northwest*—did we really need another "wrong guy" movie? And the rape scene, which may have been out of context in this type of film, hinted at the more undiluted violence that Hitch would embrace in his next actual project—*Psycho.*

And it was then, after *Psycho,* that Hitchcock developed one of the greatest movies never made from an idea by *North by Northwest* screenwriter Ernest Lehman. Titled *The Blind Man*, it was about a piano player who has been blind since birth. Medical advances make possible a double cornea transplant, and the first place the man wants to see is Disneyland. The picture takes place in Disneyland as the blind man, seeing for the first time in his life, discovers he has been given the eyes of a murdered man. He attempts to track down the killer, who in turn is trying to kill him. Jimmy Stewart was considered for the lead role.

Lehman ultimately gave up on the project because of certain plot difficulties he just didn't have the stamina to transcend and because the project seemed doomed after Walt Disney's reaction to *Psycho.*

Disney said that he wouldn't let his children see the film and certainly wouldn't let its director shoot a picture at Disneyland.

Lehman later had regrets, however. He said he wished that "someone had locked the doors and told me I couldn't leave because I still think it was a good idea and with Hitch and me hanging in to the bitter end, I might have licked the screenplay. . . . The experiences of a blind man seeing the world for the first time, it could have been a memorable film."

There are great unmade films that stalled at each and every stage of development. Some became scripts, some were partly filmed, and some—like *The Blind Man*—were little more than a story. But what a story, and in the hands of a master filmmaker like Hitchcock! A supernatural chase thriller featuring a grown man who sees the world for the first time at Disneyland . . . sublime!

Deprived of the opportunity to shoot a picture in the Enchanted Tiki Room, Hitchcock proceeded to make *The Birds*.

Bogart Slept Here

And the next to last scene of The Goodbye Girl, *wherein Richard Dreyfuss's character is asked to be in a movie, was actually the beginning of* Bogart Slept Here.

Richard Dreyfus never had the opportunity to flex his acting muscles in *Bogart Slept Here*, the proposed sequel to *The Goodbye Girl*.

In the introduction to the February 1978 *Playboy* interview with Neil Simon, readers were informed that "as we went to press . . . Simon was putting the finishing touches on his sequel to *The Goodbye Girl,* which will again star Richard Dreyfuss and Simon's wife, actress Marsha Mason."

In the November 10, 1978, *Esquire* article "Richard Dreyfuss Is out of Control," by Jean Vallely, readers were told: "And Dreyfuss is already preparing for his next role, the sequel to *The Goodbye Girl,* in which Elliot Garfield goes to Hollywood, becomes a big star, freaks out and learns to deal with his success. The movie doesn't shoot until next year, and at the moment he wants no other projects."

Reportedly, *The Goodbye Girl,* for which he won the Academy Award for Best Actor, was Dreyfuss's favorite film. He said, "I could do *The Goodbye Girl* as a nine-to-five job for the rest of my life."

For his part, Neil Simon was quoted as saying that though Dreyfuss was "not a handsome-man type like Redford or a dramatic-actor type like Pacino or De Niro, Rick can do anything—and he is funnier than any of them."

But despite the obvious enthusiasm of the principals for each other and for the project, *Mr. Famous—The Goodbye Girl* sequel—was never made.

The irony of the whole thing is that *The Goodbye Girl* was actually a prequel to *Mr. Famous,* because the original version of *Mr. Famous—Bogart Slept Here*—was written first! It was the film Neil Simon originally wanted to make. And it actually went into production before *The Goodbye Girl* was even written!

Neil Simon said, "The story of *The Goodbye Girl* is as complicated as *La Ronde. Bogart Slept Here,* which started it all, was a screenplay about success and what it does to you. I was writing from personal experiences, and not only my own; I deal with a lot of successful people and I see how it affects them. I decided to do a story about an actor who becomes an overnight success."

So Neil Simon, whose greatest plays, such as *Brighton Beach Memoirs* and *Broadway Bound,* were drawn from his own experiences, had a strong desire to express himself cinematically on the subject of success and what he and others had gone through as a result of it.

"That was the background for *Bogart Slept Here,* which was to be a film about a young New York actor who's married and has a couple of kids, and who gets this big part in a movie and goes to Hollywood."

He originally thought of Dustin Hoffman for the lead, because Hoffman had had some of the experiences that were explored in the film, but it finally went into production with Robert De Niro and Marsha Mason as the stars and Mike Nichols as director. Unfortunately, De Niro started the picture the Monday after finishing *Taxi Driver* and just couldn't seem to shake the Travis Bickle character.

"What we had on screen for seven days days was pretty grim," Simon was quoted as saying. After spending thirty to forty thousand dollars a day and getting extremely unsatisfactory results, Mike Nichols finally bit the bullet and called the whole thing off.

Said Simon, "I think Mike was very brave to do it because he was sure to get bad press for dropping a picture after having just had an unsuccessful film venture with *The Fortune*."

Executives at Warner Bros. were not as willing as Nichols to throw in the towel, so they talked to other directors about picking up where Nichols left off. Richard Dreyfuss was called in to do a reading with Marsha Mason to see if he might be right for the De Niro part. By now, however, all that had transpired had caused Neil Simon to distrust his own script. But he loved the chemistry between Mason and Dreyfuss.

"My solution was to write a different picture for them, yet I wanted to keep the character of the struggling young actor," offered Simon, "so I abandoned *Bogart Slept Here* and began writing *The Goodbye Girl*." And the next to last scene of *The Goodbye Girl*, wherein Richard Dreyfuss's character is asked to be in a movie, was actually the beginning of *Bogart Slept Here*.

"I just wrote backward from there," explained Simon, "because I wanted to write a romantic story showing how these two people meet."

Simon, who had written *Bogart Slept Here* as a significant vehicle of self-expression, actually thought of *The Goodbye Girl* as something of a trifle.

"When I wrote *The Goodbye Girl*," he said, "I thought it would be a nice little picture for Marsha and me to do together. . . . In any case, when I first saw *The Goodbye Girl* in a screening room, I really liked it, and I thought that just maybe it would make its cost back. I was sure that very few people would be interested in a picture that just told a small story."

So we see that Simon was having second thoughts about a script that meant a lot to him and then had little faith in the more frivolous prequel he subsequently wrought. "During the making of *The Goodbye Girl*," he was reported as saying, "I wanted to shelve it because it seemed light to me."

But *The Goodbye Girl* turned out to be a massive success, and Simon announced, "We'll be doing a sequel to *The Goodbye Girl* this summer. It'll be called *Mr. Famous* and I'm using *Bogart Slept Here* as the basis for the screenplay. . . . Richard's not planning to do another picture until we shoot *Mr. Famous* in July."

Marsha Mason described *Mr. Famous,* saying, "The hero became a success, had money, fame, the girl, and still wasn't happy." In many respects this sounds like contemporaneous news accounts of Richard Dreyfuss himself. Perhaps this was a project that cut a little too close to the bone for the people involved. Because on December 8, 1978, *Daily Variety*'s Army Archerd reported: "Simon  admits the sequel to *The Goodbye Girl* (*Mr. Famous*) is called off. . . . He thinks it might make 'a nice TV series.' "

Marsha Mason admitted that "Neil felt, well, people won't care about the problems of a guy who has everything and is still miserable." And Richard Dreyfuss, marching in lockstep, said, "No one gives a damn about the problems of a movie star."

And so Pulitzer Prize–winning playwright Neil Simon managed to talk himself out of making a picture about the truth of success as he had experienced it, fearing the public wouldn't accept it. If only he had remembered that he also had feared they would reject *The Goodbye Girl*. "I'm beginning to not trust what I say," he once told Army Archerd.

If Robert De Niro had been able to get in touch with his comic side or if Mike Nichols had been willing to stay the course or if Neil Simon had later trusted the public to understand the downside of showbiz triumph, we could have had one hell of a movie. But Richard Dreyfuss did not reprise his Oscar-winning character. And *Bogart Slept Here/Mr. Famous* remains one of the greatest films never made.

Bug Jack Barron

One established publisher called it "cynical, depraved, utterly degenerate; sure to be a hit with pseudo-intellectuals and the would-be literati."

Modern times seem defined in America by our willingness, even our desire, to air our dirty laundry on television. The Jerry Springer/Gerry Rivers/Jenny Jones phenomenon has brought into homes the trashiest aspects of American life. At the same time, we have elevated the interlocutors of these trash fests to the position of teacher/counselor/father/mother figures in our lives.

We call to express our frustration and rage over the radio airwaves. Rush Limbaugh and his ilk are our broadcast bartenders to whom we spill our daily problems. But when I say "our," do I really mean "their?" A goodly percentage of Americans regard the program forms of which I write as freak shows—tawdry displays of how the other "half" (90 percent?) lives. While everybody watches, it seems it is the underclass that truly "believes." To a segment of society, Springer's "advice" and "opinions" really matter, the tabloid Geraldo is equal to the newsman Geraldo, and Judge Judy is the answer to lawlessness in America.

Decades ago, TV/radio personality Arthur Godfrey was said to have great power. (*The Great Man,* a fifties film starring Jose Ferrer, was about such a demagogic broadcaster.) But has any commercial American broadcaster been a populist demagogue in the political sense? Arthur Godfrey used his power to sell Lipton tea and to keep his employees in line. Oprah Winfrey tells Americans what books to read. Jerry Springer uses his pulpit to find dates. We haven't had a good old destructive broadcast figure since the days of Father Coughlin back in the thirties.

Still, don't go around congratulating yourselves that America is immune to such manipulations. Our most imperial broadcast figures do indeed have great power. Their audiences hang onto their every word. Only a last shred of responsibility or an extremely limited worldview keeps these figures from misusing their power. If Oprah decided to use her popularity to push something destructive, there's a good chance she'd have some success. Barry Diller and Jerry Springer have differed over the direction of Springer's show, but if a Diller/Murdoch/Turner and a Springer/Jones/Whoever agreed on an agenda, they could easily manipulate the underclass (and therefore the world). In older times, such figures succeeded with speeches in Town Square, so imagine what could be done today. What if, instead of exploiting our suspicions with programming like *The X-Files*, we were exploited with "news?" (Some say we already are.) Well, some thirty years ago a premise of that sort was put forth by Norman Spinrad in his book *Bug Jack Barron*. The sixties novel posited that at some point in the future a talk show host had become so powerful that he could move a nation. His fans consisted of the poor and the disenfranchised. And his name was Bug Jack Barron. (Two out of three ain't bad!)

Spinrad gave Barron an interesting past. He was a left-wing activist who had turned cynical. His wife left him, believing him a sellout. But Barron, while cynical on the surface, was still an idealist underneath his facade. He specialized in attacking those who deserved to be attacked.

One worthy target was billionaire Benedict Howard. Howard was tied in with the big American power structures, the CIA and the like.

He headed the Foundation for Human Immortality, which, rather than perform research that would benefit all, was a cover for a cryogenic monopoly. If Howard's freezing technologies would allow humans to live forever, the beneficiaries would not be the have-nots of Barron's audience. They would be the rich and powerful, like Howard himself. In this regard, the thirty-year-old novel again parallels our own time. After all, we now have organizations sponsored by tobacco companies and gun lobbies that masquerade behind names like the People vs. Guns and Smoking. Someone is always trying to confuse the masses into endorsing positions that are dangerous to them.

Director Costa-Gavras, struck by the powerful truths of the Spinrad novel, tried during the 1980s to transfer its story to film. The director of *Z* and *Missing* had just won the Palme D'or at the Cannes Film Festival and was so enthused that he moved to LA to prepare his film. Production was tentatively scheduled for the summer of '83, and producer Ed Lewis hired Harlan Ellison to write the screenplay for the Universal release.

From the date of its creation, *Bug Jack Barron* had unnerved and threatened those living within the corridors of power. Its cynicism, extreme language, and openly sexual aspects caused an outcry in the publishing community. Distributors and bookstores refused it. One established publisher called it "cynical, depraved, utterly degenerate; sure to be a hit with pseudo-intellectuals and the would-be literati." (This quote later appeared on the cover of the book.)

Well, in hindsight, we know the sociological trends spotted by Spinrad to be absolutely real. Who knows if the publisher quoted was unaware of Spinrad's accuracy? Then, as now, such figures had reason to fear such honest prognostications.

Three producers failed in their attempts to produce the film before the abortive Costa-Gavras version, and Spinrad's own pre-Ellison screenplay remains in a drawer somewhere, covered in dust. (OK, maybe it's in a box.) I don't want to sound like Mulder here, but around the time of the Costa-Gavras version's development activist/comedian Dick Gregory was saying that missing Atlanta kids had been used in secret biological experiments and that their bodies were being disposed of publicly to suggest the work of a freelance maniac. Well, Spinrad believed such possibilities way back in '67. And Gregory had once been considered for the role of Lukas Greene, the head of the Bug Jack Barron–supported Sacred Justice Coalition.

While we don't have holo-television, in certain respects *Bug Jack Barron* told us where we were going and could have served as a warning, helped us change direction. A film version could have really left a mark.

Instead we remain firmly on course. America's power class can feel secure.

Casablanca 2

Was it really the beginning of a beautiful friendship for Rick and Captain Renault?

In 1992, at Turner Entertainment's fiftieth anniversary salute to *Casablanca*, no less lofty a presence than the official representative of the king of Morocco asked, "Wouldn't it be a wonderful thing if we could do a sequel?" And he was not alone in feeling as he did. Like most classic movies, *Casablanca* has been the subject of intense speculation. "Whatever became of Ilsa and Rick?" people ask themselves. "Did they meet again after the war?"

Would Rick and Ilsa have reunited? We'll never know since they never made *Casablanca 2*.

"Did Rick move back to America?" "Did Sam?" "Was it really the beginning of a beautiful friendship for Rick and Captain Renault?"

The only way for people to get the answers to these questions, the only way for them to know for sure, would be to see a sequel. So, as with *Gone with the Wind* and so many others, people have wished for a continuation of *Casablanca*.

There have, of course, been new "versions" of Casablanca over the years, seeking to satisfy that part of the public that wants to see "more" of their favorite characters. There was not one but *two* musical versions of the story developed, and both got pretty damn far! In 1951 and '52, for example, Australian producers worked with two of the original *Casablanca* screenwriters, Julius and Philip Epstein, and then separately worked with Alan Jay Lerner and Fritz Loewe (eventually to author such musical classics as *My Fair Lady* and *Camelot*) on a musical *Casablanca*. Despite these heavy hitters, the project never reached fruition.

Later, in 1967, Julius Epstein, having survived his brother Philip, wrote a different musical version with bigtime American songwriters Arthur Schwartz ("Dancing in the Dark," etc.) and Leo Robin. (Obviously, Epstein believed strongly in the musical potential of the story.) Executives at Seven Arts, which merged with *Casablanca* producer Warner Bros. that year, believed Epstein, Schwartz, and Robin had been "meticulously faithful" to the original film. In one musical sequence, a chorus of refugees sang a number questioning the wisdom and benefits of going to the USA. Another sequence featured a duet between Rick and Sam.

Seven Arts ultimately rejected the notion of investing in the project because it found such a seemingly whimsical permutation of the drama to be kind of ridiculous. But the studio's skittishness ignored the fact that many serious subjects have been turned into musicals with exciting and dramatic results. And the veterans who labored to produce this incarnation were no slouches. But like the previous effort, the production was never mounted.

There were two new productions of *Casablanca* mounted over the years, both of them for television. The first aired from 1955 to 1957 as part of Warner Bros.' first television series, *Warner Bros. Presents*. Aired over the American Broadcasting Company's network, the *Casablanca* series starred Charles McGraw as Rick and Marcel Dalio, who had played Rick's croupier in the original film, as Captain "Renaud." (For some reason, they changed the spelling of the captain's name.) Dan Seynour, also "promoted" from a smaller role in the original film, played the Sydney Greenstreet role. Clarence Muse, who had been considered for the part in the original, played Sam. And Ludwig Stossel replaced the original's S. Z. Sakall.

Casablanca alternated with several other series on *Warner Bros. Presents*, all of which were drawn from Warner Bros. classics with the exception of *Cheyenne*. Perhaps instructively, *Cheyenne* was the only success of the lot and ultimately became a freestanding series of its own. Still, the power of *Casablanca* was strong. Said then–Warner Bros. television head William Orr, "*Casablanca* didn't do that badly except compared to *Cheyenne*. But it never occurred to us that we could do more than one television series, so we took *Casablanca* off the air."

Casablanca was to return to the air, however, in 1983 over the NBC television network. It starred David Soul (!) of *Starsky and Hutch* and ran for only three episodes.

The same decade featured an attempt by original *Casablanca* screenwriter Howard Koch to bring forth an actual *Casablanca* sequel. In his story, Ilsa and Rick's son (!) goes to Morocco to find out what happened to his dad. Nothing of consequence, however, seems to have happened to this attempt at a sequel.

Earlier, the great French director François Truffaut had been approached about doing a remake of the original film. He admitted that he was "intimidated" by the prospect and went on to say, "I cannot imagine Jean-Paul Belmondo or Catherine Deneuve being willing to step into the shoes of Humphrey Bogart and Ingrid Bergman."

Julius Epstein said, "The reason it never works, no matter how hard they try, is that people have in their heads Bogart and Bergman. The new actors may be better, but they're not Bogart and Bergman." But what most people don't realize is that Warner Bros. actually announced a sequel to the film during its original golden era.

Brazzaville, a sequel to *Casablanca,* was announced by the studio in 1943. It was to star Bogart, Sydney Greenstreet, and Geraldine Fitzgerald as a Red Cross nurse. This version was ultimately abandoned.

Was their love great enough to spawn a sequel to *Casablanca*?

Another one, by Frederik Stephani, started at the conclusion of the original, with Inspector Renault instructing his officers to round up the usual suspects. That very night, Allied troops invade Casablanca and it turns out that Renault and Rick have been Allied operatives all along.

These multiple development efforts indicate that Warner Bros. was very serious about doing a timely sequel to the film. Had the project not gotten lost in the studio development shuffle, we could have spent more time in the company of Bogart, Rains, Greenstreet, and others in their famous and beloved roles—in glorious black and white and at the same moment in time as their original triumph. Because of the vagaries of studio development and the relative dearth of sequels in those times, we were deprived of the opportunity to do so. And so we'll have to stick with Woody Allen's famous comedy as the only true Bogart-infused "continuation" of the original story. Or we can simply continue to watch the original film over and over, as we have through the decades . . .

Play it again, Sam.

The Cradle Will Rock

*A new day had dawned in the theatre. The stagnant
and supine audience had been killed forever.*

In his midtwenties, Orson Welles directed *Citizen Kane,* believed by
many to be the greatest movie ever made. By his late sixties, the
aging wunderkind had racked up an astonishing collection of unfinished films, including *The Deep, The Big Brass Ring, The Dreamers, It's
All True,* and *The Other Side of the Wind.* In 1984, just weeks from
starting what may have been the greatest movie never made by the
director of the greatest movie ever made, Welles found his financing
suddenly and permanently withdrawn. But the story of *The Cradle
Will Rock* actually began some five decades earlier, during the 1930s.
The original *The Cradle Will Rock* was a "people's opera" by composer
Marc Blitzstein, produced during the Great Depression by the Federal
Theatre Project.

The Federal Theatre Project was a division of the Works Progress
Administration (WPA), which had been created by Franklin Delano
Roosevelt to provide work for the many Americans who were un-
employed. Then, as now, America's political right was opposed to
government subsidization of the arts as well as to work programs of
a more conventional nature because they represented "creeping socialism." But in pre–World War II, pre–cold war, depression-scarred

America, there was much enthusiasm for socialism, creeping or otherwise. And so it was that under the auspices of the U.S. government a musical play that praised unionism and socialism while damning the military, the judicial system, American industry, and the press was directed by a pre–*Citizen Kane* Orson Welles. Though at this point in Welles's career even his radio adaptation of *War of the Worlds* was still in the future, he had recently gained notoriety for his direction of a voodoo-themed production of *Macbeth* with an all-black cast. His producer on that project had been John "They Earn It" Houseman, and it was with Houseman that Welles embarked upon the production of this, his first musical.

The great composer Aaron Copland called the *The Cradle Will Rock*'s author, Marc Blitzstein, "the first American composer to invent a vernacular musical idiom that sounded convincing when heard on the lips of the man-in-the street." And Blitzstein was plenty impressed with director Welles, later remembering him as "only 21, but already a . . . brilliant theatre man." The play took place in Steeltown, USA, and had characters with names like Harry Druggist, Dr. Specialist, the Rev. Salvation, Editor Daily, President Prexy, and Mr. Mister. Almost all were corrupt tools of the capitalist system. (An early version of the script featured a worker and a farmer named Mr. Hammer and Mr. Sickle.) Young Welles prepared an extravagant production of this extremely ideological material.

But on June 10, 1937, just four days before the show was scheduled to open, the government ordered the budget of the Federal Theatre Project cut by 30 percent. Approximately seventeen hundred workers were to be let go, and no plays were to open before July 11. Welles, with a finished production all set to open, begged the government to permit him to open the show, but the answer was a cold, hard "no."

Like a convicted murderer awaiting a reprieve from the governor, Welles angled for a way out. On "opening night," audience members gathered outside the locked-up theater. Will "Grandpa Walton" Geer and Howard "Ben Franklin" Da Silva entertained them in the street while Welles and his collaborators tried to extract themselves from their predicament. They considered leasing another theater and producing the show commercially, but the financial demands of the actors' and musicians' unions rendered this course of action impractical. The survival of this pro-union show was being imperiled by the demands of the unions.

In the street, pamphlets were handed out that read: "Your friends have been dismissed. You could be next." Welles and Houseman decided that they would rent a theater regardless of the union demands and announced to the actors that the union would not allow them to perform from the stage, but that they were free to buy tickets and speak from the audience if they desired. The cast, creators, and audience members then "marched" the few blocks to the new theater wherein, accompanied by the composer at the piano, the actors performed the entire show as members of the audience!

Among those present was poet Archibald MacLeish, who excitedly stated that "a new day had dawned in the theatre. The stagnant and supine audience had been killed forever."

The press reports of this guerrilla production created a commercial demand. The sets that were constructed for the production as originally intended had been smashed by the WPA, but this was not a problem, as the play was presented for the rest of its run as it had been on opening night—from the audience!

Welles went on to other triumphs, but the story of *The Cradle Will Rock* loomed large in the memories of those who had experienced and been affected by it. Eventually, screenwriter Ring Lardner Jr. (who had been blacklisted during the McCarthy era for his leftist past, but whose later triumphs include the screenplay for *M*A*S*H*) decided to recount the legendary saga for the benefit of modern audiences. Orson Welles was asked to direct.

At first Welles was cold to the idea, feeling the Welles of a half-century earlier was a stranger to him. But eventually he became enthused by the chance to present himself and his life from the vantage point of what he had become. Rupert Everett was cast as Welles, and

Amy Irving was to play the female lead. Shooting would be done in Rome. At the last minute, the financier dropped out when he realized that a major distributor was not attached to the film. Welles looked to his young Hollywood friends for help. He begged Warren Beatty and Jack Nicholson to assist him, but it was to no avail. They told him he was his own worst enemy.

Welles figured they told themselves that so that they would not feel guilty when they refused to help him. However, he believed that he had an "ace in the hole." After all, his leading lady, Amy Irving, was involved with Steven Spielberg, whom Welles called Mr. Moneybags.

Irving, Spielberg, and Welles went to dinner together, but it was to no avail. During dinner, Spielberg spoke of Welles's career entirely in the past tense. Welles was heartbroken. He would never get to use the special effects he had commissioned from a group of talented magicians. He told one biographer, "I cannot think of who is going to pay those people who trusted me." He lived another year or so, doing his commercial voice-overs and vaudevillian-type guest appearances. But he never got the chance to craft his late-life ruminations on his youthful triumph. And we, the audience, are the losers.

In this particular case, however, all is not lost, for Tim Robbins is making his own version from a modern perspective. It's not Welles, but it's something.

Dean Martin

*Scorsese apparently would rather wait forever than
go ahead without the involvement of John Travolta
as Sinatra, Hugh Grant as Peter Lawford, Adam
Sandler as Joey Bishop, and Jim Carrey as Jerry
Lewis.*

When Frank Sinatra died, Dean Martin's ex-wife Jeanne said that
while Dean had more hit records during the Rat Pack era than
Swoonatra did, she never harbored any doubts about whose musical
legacy would live forever. She added that Frank cared about being a
musical artist, but that Dean just cared about being funny.

But funny is good. And just a few years after his death, Dean Martin
has firmly returned to the center of cool. The hip lifestyle embodied
by the Rat Pack is back in vogue. Ain't that a kick in the head?

Unlike Elvis, who once idolized him, Drunky Dean did not die
young. He lived beyond the biblical three score and ten, without any
special evidence that he had taken care of himself. He even died cool,
first receding from public view just because he wanted to. And so
Dino is living larger in death than he did in life.

Cut to Martin Scorsese, another Italian-American, who's been livin'
large in his own manner, regarded by many as one of the great American directors. He's known primarily for bloody, violent films like

Martin Scorsese has wanted to bring the story of the life of Dean Martin to the screen for years.

Martin Scorsese still dreams of making a film about the life of Dean Martin.

Mean Streets, GoodFellas, Taxi Drivers, and *Raging Bull,* but many forget that he has directed musicals, historical films, comedies, and documentaries. When it was announced that Scorsese would direct a film of the star's life, many reacted as if that was odd. But Dean and Scorsese are connected by more than just the name Martin.

For instance, there's the star of Scorsese's *King of Comedy*—Dean's ex-partner, Jerry Lewis. Scorsese told an audience in Ireland how he had chosen Lewis for the piece: "And we did speak to Carson and he didn't really want to go into acting in any way, so then we thought of different people, thought of Dean Martin even, a wonderful actor, great singer, great personality. But I said, what about Jerry Lewis; he's not only a comic, but he does monologues, directs, is a humanitarian, does that incredible telethon, which many people criticize but at the same time raises a lot of money, and that sort of thing. That showbusiness edge, Jerry Lewis has all of that."

If the infamous Kevin Bacon Six Degrees of Separation game featured Martin Scorsese, the director and Dean could be connected in two degrees and from sixty directions.

Dean co-starred with Scorsese actor Joe Pesci on the eighties TV series *Half-Nelson*. Scorsese dated Liza Minnelli and directed her on stage and film, and she's the performer who replaced Martin in the Rat Pack reunion tour later in the eighties. No matter how different, show business personalities are never far removed from one another—remember that Mia Farrow was lover to Frank Sinatra *and* Woody Allen both.

But when you're at the center of the show biz maelstrom you don't always recognize your connections to the others in your field. (It may be a trifle difficult, for instance, for a Robert De Niro to acknowledge that, to some degree, he's in the same business as Pat Sajak.) So, when Warner Bros., having purchased Nick Tosches's, book about the crooner, offered Scorsese the reins to the Martin picture, the director was uncertain.

But he came around.

As he told the Irish crowd, ". . . the studio presented me with

Left to right: John Travolta would have played Frank Sinatra in Martin Scorsese's film about the life of Dean Martin, Hugh Grant as Peter Lawford, Adam Sandler as Joey Bishop, and Jim Carrey as Jerry Lewis.

the idea of Dean Martin, which I was reluctant to do at first, but then I realized that's again a period I grew up around, the late forties, early fifties. I loved Dean Martin and Jerry Lewis. When I was in my teens I adored the Rat Pack idea. But it takes me a little while to pull a picture together. Nick Pileggi and myself are working on a script on Dean Martin, and it has more to do with American celebrity, creating an image. Because his real name is Dino Crocetti and it becomes Dean Martin. Cuts his nose to fit into American society. And so in a funny way it's about hiding behind an image. And then never being able to get past it. You know, and then also having enough; he had enough money and he just didn't want to play anymore. He wasn't interested. There's that element; that interests me there."

And that's the take that Scorsese and his *GoodFellas* collaborator Nicholas Pileggi decided to pursue for the picture. Scorsese had been collaborating with Paul (*Taxi Driver*) Schrader on a film about a New York Emergency Medical Service driver and had also been developing a George Gershwin biopic and a documentary on Italian cinema when he accepted the Dean Martin assignment. To him, it seemed the likeliest to go forward. In the first half of 1998, as Pileggi worked on the second draft of the script, the elements started to fall into place, so it seemed as if Scorsese was right.

Time magazine announced that John Travolta would likely play Sinatra in the picture; then Travolta acknowledged that he would. Scorsese himself said flat out that Tom Hanks would play Dean Martin. Frank Sinatra's death in June only heightened interest in the film. True, HBO was making its own Rat Pack picture, but they didn't have a Martin Scorsese at the helm and they weren't focusing on Martin and they were on television and they . . . Well, you know the routine.

So it came as something of a shock when it was announced on July 30, 1998, that the film was not going to be made.

Daily Variety's Army Archerd reported that it was Scorsese himself who had made the decision because of difficulties acquiring his "dream cast." Scorsese apparently would rather wait forever than go ahead without the involvement of John Travolta as Sinatra, Hugh Grant as Peter Lawford, Adam Sandler as Joey Bishop, and Jim Carrey as Jerry Lewis.

Archerd reported that "all of them are currently busy in projects taking them well into the year (and next)." Archerd further reported that "instead of starting the Martin biopic, Scorsese will probably next direct *Bringing Out the Dead* starring Nicolas Cage."

Ah, the movie business. The Dean Martin picture would have allowed Scorsese to straddle the worlds of *Casino, King of Comedy, New York, New York,* and *Mean Streets* via the life and persona of an American entertainment giant. Instead we get another Nicolas Cage movie.

Now that's a kick in the head.

.

Destino

The most intriguing Disney film was a planned collaboration between Walt Disney and noted surrealist Salvador Dalí.

There are a ton of Disney projects that never saw the light of day, and many of them were very interesting. There were many other intriguing Disney notions that went unfulfilled. Features were developed to star Mickey, Donald, and Goofy, which would have been the animated equivalent of the feature-length work of live-action comedians who started in shorts, like Laurel and Hardy. There was a live action/animation version of *Hans Christian Andersen* that was developed to a very significant degree and which would have involved that other great producer with his name on his studio, Samuel Goldwyn. And Disney at one time pursued the Babar the Elephant stories.

Chanticleer, the story of the self-focused rooster who thinks his crowing make the sun rise, was another project developed by the studio over a period of many years. (The story was eventually animated a few years ago by Disney refugee Don Bluth, under the title *Rock-a Doodle*.)

Of course, I'm not talking about Disney, the corporate monolith that we know today; I'm talking about Disney, the little studio during the golden age of Hollywood. It's no accident that unlike Paramount or Universal, Disney is a studio that bears a single man's name. During its formative period (and we're talking about decades here), the output of that little studio clearly reflected the vision of that one man.

The most intriguing Disney film was a planned collaboration between Walt Disney and noted surrealist Salvador Dalí. It might sound like a strange combination—the conservative Disney and the outré Dalí—but remember, Disney was at one time positively out there in terms of innovation. Forget about *Fantasia*—even the straight-ahead, ultra-"realistic" rendering in "conventional" Disney cartoons was unprecedented in the motion picture medium at the time.

Meanwhile, Dalí had already worked on more than one film project, including an attempted collaboration with the Marx Brothers. Indeed, it was while Dalí was working on a dream sequence for Alfred Hitchcock's *Spellbound* that he and Disney came together. Regardless, even at the time people were freaked out by the notion of the Disney/Dalí collaboration. "Disney and Dalí Join for Weird Film Opus" and "Masters of Mickey Mouse and Limp Watch Team Up" were but two of the articles that appeared while the project was under development.

Disney, rankling at the thought that he should be strait jacketed into one stylistic mode, told the press he was put off by "people who try to keep me in well-worn grooves." He felt he had to go on "breaking new trails." He noted that *Fantasia* had been criticized upon its release, but that it had grown in popularity (as it has continued to do ever since).

The Disney/Dalí film was to be called *Destino*. It was to be of less than feature length and would have been released along with other material. It was to mix live-action and animation in a story of young lovers who battle various impediments to fulfill their love for each other. Judging from the surviving materials, *Destino* (to have been accompanied by Armando Dominguez's ballad of the same name) was intended to eschew traditional narrative structure. From Dalí we could expect no less.

Dalí himself considered appearing in the film. He was to have explained that surrealism is akin to a new language composed of symbols and, as a result, nothing is what it would ordinarily appear to be. He would have further explained that his famous limp watch (visible on an easel alongside him) symbolized the relativity of time— how some events make time go faster while others make it feel slower. "Mechanical time" would be proclaimed as different from the kind of time experienced by human beings. This would of course lead into the animation of Dalí's surrealistic images. Ballet star Andre Eglevsky was under consideration to appear in the love/dance segment of the film, while the animated images were to have included such visual notions as infinite rocky regions, stretched-out characters, structures in ruins, and telephones with spider legs.

Representing a kind of conventional wisdom that stands in the way of the female lover's happiness, she was to have been chased by pursuers with eyeballs instead of heads. Another sequence would have featured the lovers in a sort of baseball dance. Dalí is reported to have been fascinated by baseball, though he claimed to know nothing at all about the game. Similarly, Dalí apparently had no particular interest in "Destiny," the song for which the film was named. He just liked the idea of destiny.

Unfortunately, the picture was never made because of changes in the Disney company's overall plans. Disney, however, referred to Dalí as "a very swell guy, and a person whom I enjoyed working with." Disney also said, "Ordinarily good story ideas don't come easy and have to be fought for, but with Dalí, it was exactly the reverse. He constantly bubbled with new ideas."

A 17-second animation test was made for the film (it featured distorted heads on tortoise shells), and that's as far as it got. Disney tried to arrange another collaboration during the fifties, but nothing came of it. (They remained friends, however, and visited each other's homes.) Still, the Disney/Dalí opus is the unfinished entry for which we should pine.

Movies mostly just try to keep the colors between the lines (so to speak). But Walt Disney, who gave us the modern animated short and the animated feature film, and Salvador Dalí, who was a prime figure in a major artistic movement, were genuine visionaries. Whatever they committed to film would have been heartfelt, authentic art. The public might have been confused, but—as with *Fantasia*—we would have eventually understood.

Some artists help keep the species moving forward, and you just don't find a lot of them in the movie business. Walt Disney and Salvador Dalí were that kind of force: at their best, both candy and spinach—sweet-tasting *and* good for you.

The Disappearance

. . . one day women disappear from the Earth. The men are all alone, except for the fact that women are really still around; they've just been caught in some kind of dimensional shift.

George Pal is well known to animation lovers as the producer/ director of the Puppetoons shorts of the thirties and forties. He is equally well-known to sci-fi fans as the producer and/or director of such classics as *Destination Moon, War of the Worlds*, and *The Time Machine*. Pulp fans hailed his *Doc Savage: The Man of Bronze*. Families flocked to see the breathtaking special effects in *Tom Thumb* and *The Wonderful World of the Brothers Grimm* (in Cinerama). All of these films were well within the attitudinal framework of the Hollywood in which he had thrived. But as far back as the 1950s, Pal harbored a desire to create a more sophisticated film—a film that looked forward, as did *The Time Machine*, but that looked inward as well, with the uncompromising eye of a social critic.

Philip Wylie, whose novel *When Worlds Collide* was transferred by Pal to the silver screen, had a filmography even more eclectic than Pal's. Wylie had supplied the screenplays or stories for such diverse productions as *Springtime in the Rockies*, starring Glenn Miller (1942),

Charlie Chan in Reno (1939), and *Murders in the Zoo* (1933). In 1950, Wylie's novel *The Disappearance* had been published and Pal immediately saw its motion picture potential.

The Disappearance was an honest, adult story in the days when the House Un-American Activities Committee was just beginning its destructive anti-Communist reign, when the "Ozzie and Harriet" fifties were about to break through in force. That Pal was so enthusiastic about this story in 1951 is astonishing.

On the other hand, Pal was a European, and in matters of art European sensibilities have long been broader than our own. Yes, Pal had played by the rules here, but so had Fritz Lang and all the other successful European expatriates in Hollywood. The fact remains that whatever the quality of their American output, their European work was generally more idiosyncratic in one way or another.

Pal's background was in animated puppets. His hard work was employed in the interest of making children of all ages smile. He was, however, a man, and few men, certainly few artists, are about one thing only. A man like George Pal, who wrote, directed, produced, and even photographed films, had to be something of a sophisticated thinker, and at some point he decided he'd like to get his more sophisticated thoughts captured on film. *The Disappearance* could have been his vehicle.

The basic premise of *The Disappearance* is that one day women disappear from the Earth. The men are all alone, except for the fact that women are really still around; they've just been caught in some kind of dimensional shift. From their perspective, it's the men who have vanished. Both men and women, seemingly without counterpart in the world they had known together, proceed to experience what the world would be if they were alone.

In the men-only world, anarchy erupts. The Russians start World War III; the streets are filled with violent mobs. In the women-only world, planes crash; essential equipment is unattended.

Men are like animals without the sensitizing influence of women.

Women have never been trained to operate mechanisms considered within the masculine domain. Because of training and/or nature, neither gender can sustain society without the other's presence.

But *The Disappearance* is more than just a variant of the "postapocalyptic" genre in literature and film. The 1951 novel predicts feminism and its theoretical underpinnings and embraces Eastern religion as a means of reconciling the physical and spiritual worlds. It's a hippie opus in the early days of the Beats, a seventies sociopolitical tract in the time of the Korean War.

The women open up nightclubs at which they release pent-up sexuality by viewing erotic shows and engaging in lesbianism. They utilize life-size love dolls (some based on celebs). There are women who start a suicide club.

A male hero, surrounded by lawlessness and antiestablishment rioting, retreats to his home and builds a Buddhist implement. His spiritual focus enables him to see that women are still there. His Zen concentration enables the two genders to become reunited. Pal said of the tale, "I don't consider this to be science fiction. I regard it as a meaningful *what if* story."

He first optioned the novel in 1951, but Paramount's Y. Frank Freeman was put off by the piece's sexuality and provocative take on religion. King Vidor and others attempted to develop the picture during the fifties, but Pal reacquired the rights sometime after moving to MGM, and the picture was announced by Metro in 1965. Unfortunately, the indecisive and impermanent MGM management turned down multiple scripts, and Pal ultimately took the project with him when he made a deal with CBS's film arm in 1968.

The movie would have featured the (not-yet-familiar) destruction of world capitals. Rioting mobs were to have been filmed on isolated highways between Florida and the Keys. There would have been psychedelic sounds and images—sitar music and a revolving Buddhist mandala.

Pal was still actively planning the film around the time of his death in 1980. He felt very strongly about the story, which shed light on our society's objectification of women and attacked the repression associated with Christian "morality." The separation of the sexes in *The Disappearance* was a form of divine intervention, and the moral of the story was that man and woman have to find/know each other in order to survive. Pal said that "a man and a woman are but half a unit and the love of a man and a woman makes the whole." He believed "*The Disappearance* will be one of the best, if not the best, pictures I have ever had the good fortune to be associated with."

The Hungarian-born film artist died from a heart attack on May 2, 1980, while his movie *The Voyage of the Berg* was in production. It remains unfinished and unreleased, but it got further than *The Disappearance,* which is still missing in inaction.

The Dreyfus Affair

Lefcourt imagined that if two baseball players were caught having a homosexual love affair it would tear America apart, just as the Dreyfus affair tore France apart.

What became known as "the Dreyfus affair" polarized France in 1894 after a high official of the French army leaked information to the Germans, signing his memo with the initial D. The espionage had actually been committed by a man known as Count Esterhazy, but the highest-ranking French officer whose name began with a D was accused. His name was Alfred Dreyfus.

Dreyfus was plagued in his quest for justice by the anti-Semitism that was—in practice—acceptable at the time. He was given a sham trial, convicted, and sent to Devil's Island. (He was eventually exonerated.)

Fascinated by the affair, Peter Lefcourt wrote a satiric novel entitled *The Dreyfus Affair* about a parallel situation in modern times. Lefcourt felt that homophobia filled the same spot in our society that anti-Semitism filled in French society a hundred years ago. He noted that even "nice" people make antigay jokes and that there is an undercurrent of discomfort with homosexuality throughout America. Lefcourt imagined that if two baseball players were caught having a homosexual love affair it would tear America apart, just as the Dreyfus affair tore France apart. He chose the baseball motif, he told an interviewer, because "baseball players are idolized in this country—they're considered role models and kids look up to them." He considered baseball "a little more Norman Rockwell's America than football or other sports." He went on to explain that "when Martina Navratilova came out of the closet, [nobody cared] much, because 1) she was a woman, 2) she was a foreigner, and 3) she was a tennis player." He also felt that organized baseball was as conservative as the French military of the nineteenth century.

Lefcourt, a novelist, playwright, and television writer, was asked to adapt his novel for the movies by producers Wendy Dozoretz and Ellen Collett, with the approval of Jeffrey Katzenberg, then at Disney. He took about three months to write the first draft.

Lefcourt took pains to make the lead character an authentic big-time jock, with a blond baseball wife and two lovely children. When Randy Dreyfus is caught having an affair with teammate D. J. Pickett, a scandal erupts that sweeps across America. Dreyfus was an icon—he even had a shopping center dedicated to him—and America has trouble believing he can be the guy they admired and also be gay. (To add another level of turmoil to the mix, Lefcourt also made the D. J. Pickett character black, simply to increase conflict.) There is a reporter named Milt Zola, who is patterned after Émile Zola, the man who publicized the Dreyfus affair in France. The president of the United States plays a part.

Unfortunately, when you're dealing with a studio there's a homogenization that takes place in even the best situations. There's a funny sequence in the book in which an exasperated Randy tries to have his dog killed. (I know it sounds horrible, but trust me; it works—just don't try it at home.) According to one account, the studio said: "You can't like anybody who kills his dog; how do you expect the audience to root for this guy?" Lefcourt replied, "Well you've never had a dalmatian." (Actually, Disney has 101 of them.) Regardless, the scene was gone.

Similarly, the studio didn't like Molly and Dolly as the names of Randy's twin daughters. They especially didn't like the fact that Randy kept mixing up their names. "How can an audience like a guy who can't tell the difference between his daughters?" they reportedly asked.

That's the problem with movie executives. They're constantly worried about how to make the audience *like* a movie's characters. The fact is, with movies—as with life—people are capable of liking characters who have any number of personality defects. The novel was out, and readers had already demonstrated that they liked the guy. Case closed.

Still, the changes from page to stage, so to speak, were relatively minor, and some may have improved the final product. Regardless, after three drafts Lefcourt's script was put into turnaround. (Turnaround is when a studio decides not to make a picture. Another studio can take it over, usually for what the first studio has already spent.) Lefcourt told an interviewer, "I think when this project was put into turnaround at Disney, the entire publicity department heaved a huge sigh of relief."

But the project wasn't finished. Some overtures were classic in their laughability. Garth Brooks, for instance, was interested in doing the film, but only if the main character wasn't gay. Barbra Streisand was interested in the project but was seemingly too involved with other pursuits. When Andrew Fleming, whose *Threesome* had done well at Sundance, became attached, *The Dreyfus Affair* regained momentum until *Threesome* opened to indifference at the box office.

Just when things looked dark, Disney was interested again.

Touchstone Pictures had previously developed the project. Now Hollywood Pictures (Disney's other grown-up label) was weighing in with an offer. David Frankel, the writer/director of *Miami Rhapsody,* wanted to direct the project, and so it was on track again. Lefcourt said he was told, ". . . this time, we're going to make it."

Well, they didn't make it. Lefcourt has speculated that Disney's purchase of the Anaheim Angels was the final nail in the coffin. Disney was actually in the baseball business now. Frankel had written a draft of the script that Lefcourt felt might have been more faithful to the book than his own had been. It languishes along with the other drafts.

Most reviews of the book noted that it was perfectly written to be translated to the screen. I recommend you pick up the novel and see the movie in your head. Just don't soil the pages with the butter from your popcorn—especially, if it's a library book.

The Elmo Aardvark Story

Many readers and the industry believed that Elmo was the first animated cartoon character, predating Mickey Mouse himself.

The late animator Shamus Culhane complained that movie executives didn't understand the hit-and-miss nature of cartoon creation. He said their attitude was something along the lines of, "Create another Bugs Bunny." It galled him that they didn't understand that you can't make a star animated character happen—you have to find him; he has to evolve.

An exception to this rule is Elmo Aardvark. During the 1990s, most everyone who has encountered the classic bow-tied picture of the character has been instantly entranced and motivated to run with the Elmo Aardvark ball. When I first saw the character in 1993, I was editing *Wild Cartoon Kingdom* magazine and decided to run a series of satirical articles about his place in animation history. I even convinced the likable film historian Leonard Maltin to provide quotes embellishing Elmo's history. Many readers and the industry believed that Elmo was the first animated cartoon character, predating Mickey Mouse himself.

Dr. Demento heard the recent Elmo Aardvark compact disc and immediately began playing its tunes. Similarly, when high-ranking Nickelodeon executives saw a picture of Elmo hanging in VP Jerry Beck's office they immediately asked, "What's that?!" and decided to pursue the character for their fledgling film division.

Will Ryan, who had been developing the character on his own, had been president of the Hollywood branch of the International Animated Film Society and was a versatile player in the animation industry. He had been the voice of numerous characters, from Disney's *Pegleg Pete* to ABC *Weekend Specials'* Morris the Moose. Ryan had been a director of development at Churchill Films, producing the pilot *Commander Toad in Space.* His recorded work included the album *Going Quackers,* which he co-wrote and on which he appeared with then-partner Phil Baron and the legendary Clarence Nash as Donald Duck.

Ryan had just released his album of Elmo Aardvark tunes when the call came from Nickelodeon

Early pencil sketches of the rascally Elmo the Aardvark.

Even though a mockumentary about Elmo was never produced, a CD of music was actually made.

Movies regarding their interest in the Elmo Aardvark character. He instructed his attorney to commence negotiations and teamed up with writer Phil Lollar to prepare a treatment for the project per Nickelodeon's instructions.

Ryan and Lollar, creator of the popular radio show *Adventures in Odyssey* (on which Ryan co-starred), conjured a truly great vehicle for their animated aardvark. In keeping with Elmo's established nature as a representative of the entirety of animation history, they decided to do a "mockumentary" that would enable them to make new cartoons featuring the aardvark in every animation style that had ever been. From Elmo's origins in the prefilm era through the silent days, the depression, World War II, early television, and the degradations of the limited animation era of the 1970s, we would experience parody, homage, and straight-ahead recreation on a feature budget. The larger budget of a feature meant that unlike tribute/parodies that had been done by such television programs as *2 Stupid Dogs* and *Animaniacs,* the new Elmo "classics" could be made with the same attention to detail as the films made during cartoondom's golden era. In addition, much of the film would feature live-action interviews meaning a higher amount of money per minute of animation would be available than for a 100 percent animated film.

This style sheet was made for the Elmo epic, *Hula Dancers.*

Promotional art was prepared by Leslie Cabarga, author of *The Fleischer Story* and one of the finest contemporary exponents of (non-Disney) thirties cartoon character design. Potential celebrity participants were approached, with a particular emphasis on personalities who would bring a period authenticity to their reminiscences. Because of the musical orientation of the project, Fayard Nicholas of the dancing Nicholas Brothers, sixties song stylist Joanie Sommers, and

Weird Al Yankovich were among those who expressed interest in the Elmo project. Consideration was also given to including contemporary rock acts paying tribute to Elmo's influence. Animation greats such as Jiminy Cricket creator Ward Kimball were expected to contribute a large portion of the historical testimony as well.

Ryan and Lollar, despite the slow pace of negotiations with Nickelodeon, turned in a treatment based on their prior discussions with the organization. Unfortunately, Nick representatives kept coming up with "new" and "different" ideas. Someone wanted the film to end with an elderly version of Elmo reuniting with his lost love, Zelma—completely ignoring the ageless nature of classic animated characters. Regardless, Ryan and Lollar did their best to adapt to the new requirements without betraying the basic nature of the film.

Elmo Aardvark from the Snappytoon, *Elmo's Big Date.*

Unfortunately, there were other aspects of this "development hell" that proved especially ruinous. Nickelodeon Movies' development process was glacially slow. From 1994, when the project started, to the present, the company has released a total of three movies, and only one of them (*The Rugrats Movie*—based on an existing Nick show and actually produced by Klasky-Csupo) was animated. Nickelodeon has no ability to make anything without the approval of sister company Paramount, through which their films are released. As a result, much of their effort is mere wheel spinning and with little need for haste.

The slow negotiations for an option on the project meant that it was essentially being developed for free. Progress would be made; then a Nick rep would go on a lengthy vacation. Suddenly there would be someone else to negotiate with as if from scratch. Frustrated, Ryan took the project to an enthusiastic Turner Feature Animation, only to see Turner swallowed up by Warner Bros., which had their own Bugs Bunny.

Facing reality, Ryan suspended the project and became a writer/producer for Nickelodeon's *Wubbulous World of Dr. Seuss*. (Yeah, I know, but it was a different part of Nickelodeon and he was actually working for Jim Henson Productions.) He's currently working with Baer Animation, which produced the Toontown section of *Who Framed Roger Rabbit?*, on a television iteration of his beloved Elmo Aardvark.

Development as used in the motion picture industry can be just another word for *frustration*. In this case, as in so many others, the development process crystallized a terrific project and then abandoned it. Suddenly, a realized blueprint for a project existed and was heartbreakingly tossed away. What kind of business is it that develops projects to the point at which their greatness becomes clear and then refuses to proceed with them?

Television has given a modern version of the animated short an opportunity to enter a second golden age. From *Ren & Stimpy,* to *The Simpsons,* to *King of the Hill,* to *South Park,* there have been high-quality projects and styles unparalleled in television history. Likewise, the Disney model for feature animation has been revived and expanded upon. But traditional comic theatrical animation remains in limbo. *The Elmo Aardvark Story* would have built a bridge to the future by joyously, comically, and lovingly evoking America's cartoon past. With its component style, it—more than anything since Roger Rabbit—could have demonstrated the contemporary viability of the theatrical short cartoon.

It's not just filmmakers and projects that get trapped in development hell. We all do.

E.R.N.

Eleanor Roosevelt's Niggers (E.R.N.) composed the 761st Tank Battalion of Gen. George S. Patton's Third Army during World War II.

Stanley Kramer has long been regarded as a filmmaker with a social conscience. His career as a producer and/or director began in the 1940s and included such classics as *The Men* (Brando's first film), *The Caine Mutiny, High Noon,* and *Inherit the Wind.* After some thirty years of fighting the good fight, Kramer therefore deserved the break he received when—upon concluding 1979's *The Runner Stumbles*—he left Hollywood for the rainy pleasures of Seattle, Washington.

Stanley Kramer worked tirelessly to bring *E.R.N.* to the screen, but it was not to be.

In Seattle, Kramer wrote a newspaper column, hosted a TV show about movies, and taught classes—in each case giving others the benefits of what he, in his long career, had learned. By 1986, however,

Kramer was ready to return to the Hollywood salt mines and go back to work. He moved back to Los Angeles and began to deal once more.

At some point, Kramer hooked up with British producer David Puttnam, who agreed to produce with Kramer a film called *Chernobyl,* about the Russian nuclear accident. Puttnam subsequently became head of Columbia Pictures, and in 1987 Kramer signed a multipicture deal with Columbia that would include *Chernobyl.* Kramer's deal was to run concurrently with Puttnam's—if Puttnam was to leave Columbia, Kramer would be finished, too.

And that's just how it went down—Puttnam left Columbia after a widely reported falling-out with the Hollywood establishment, and his replacement, the late Dawn Steel, dropped the picture. "Hollywood hasn't changed," said Kramer, "because I made a deal with David Puttnam and David Puttnam is leaving Columbia."

There were other projects that Kramer hustled to make. Warner Bros. dropped *Polonaise,* about the Polish Solidarity movement and its leader, Lech Walesa, due to legal difficulties regarding rights. And *The Bubble Man,* which Kramer was to make for Trimark around 1991, likewise never happened.

When Brandon Tartikoff was running Paramount, he looked at a whole stack of Kramer projects that had never been made, with an eye toward finding a lost Kramer gem. One of the most luminescent of those unproduced gems was *Sheiks of Araby,* which had been planned in 1966 as a sequel to Kramer's *It's a Mad, Mad, Mad, Mad World.* The early-nineties plan for the project was to bring back the survivors of the original enterprise, such as Milton Berle, Sid Caesar, Buddy Hackett, Mickey Rooney, and Carl Reiner and unite them with newer comics like Richard Lewis, Roseanne, and Robin Williams. *Mad World* veteran Jonathan Winters was to have appeared as every dictator in the world.

Unfortunately, this, too, never came to pass.

For some reason, when a Hollywood player lets his momentum flag it's often hard to get it going again. Kramer's seven years away from the game had changed the configuration of the board, and others were now more adept at the game. Perhaps there was also the long-standing Hollywood prejudice against older players and/or the fact that younger players may well have been intimidated by Kramer's reputation. The fact remains that despite the great man's efforts, none of these movies ever got made.

And the greatest of Kramer's unmade movies of the eighties and nineties may well have been *E.R.N.*

Eleanor Roosevelt's Niggers (E.R.N.) composed the 761st Tank Battalion in Gen. George S. Patton's Third Army during World War II. They gave themselves their nickname because Mrs. Roosevelt had campaigned for their right to go into combat despite resistance from Patton and other officials who wanted blacks to undertake only incidental military roles. They fought valiantly and lost a lot of men during the Battle of the Bulge. Though relatively little attention was paid them over the years, they were true pioneers, since the army was segregated until 1948. Pres. Jimmy Carter gave them the Presidential Unit Citation for gallant combat service 30 years later, in 1978.

Kramer was the perfect producer/director to make this film, as his production of *Home of the Brave* in 1949 had featured one of the earliest filmic depictions of the black soldiers' difficulties during World War II. Kramer had also made the race relations landmark *The Defiant Ones,* in which Sidney Poitier and Tony Curtis were shackled together as escaped members of a chain gang. And his *Guess Who's Coming to Dinner* (also with Poitier) was a landmark comic study of interracial marriages. Kramer had grown in the intervening years, and now gone was the paternalism of the earlier era.

"I now know," he said, "the black man must create his own destiny. I never was a good spokesman for the black man through four films, because I was a white man." Regardless, Kramer wanted to "do what they do, to walk in their shoes" while making *E.R.N.*

E.R.N.'s impending production was announced in 1990. It was to be based on a book by David J. Williams, who was the white commanding officer of the 761st. The film was to have been shot in the

South and in Europe and was to be produced by a production company co-owned by Robert Guillaume. (He was not to have acted in the film.) The funding was solicited from private sources in the United States and Europe. Kramer felt the funding was so solid that they didn't need a preproduction distribution deal, although he said, "If anybody wants to talk, we'll talk."

There were to be seven or eight black leads and one white, for whom Kramer wanted Tom Hanks. Eleanor Roosevelt's Niggers were to have used their nickname in a song they were to sing during the climactic firefight over a Belgian bridge. The film was to express "the humor of a man in a position where he's got no other defense mechanism."

Kramer explained that the men of the 761st were "trying to reverse the concept voiced by General Patton and others that blacks weren't fit for combat." The 761st actually rioted over the denial of their right to be sent into combat, and Kramer felt that the film would have more resonance than the similarly themed Civil War picture *Glory,* because the setting was more modern and, unlike the black characters in *Glory,* the 761st "did it themselves. They forced themselves into combat."

Kramer, the winner of many awards for his films and his social conscience, never won an Oscar. "Maybe this is the one," he said of *E.R.N.* But it was not.

One of the films producers said that the attempt to make *E.R.N.* involved "less than pleasant struggles." He said there was a "resistance factor to the picture that was very strong and in some respect still is."

And so a veteran filmmaker's golden opportunity fell apart due to the difficulties of trying to mount a tough film in the post–golden age, post–*Star Wars* era. To date, 1979's *The Runner Stumbles* remains Stanley Kramer's last film.

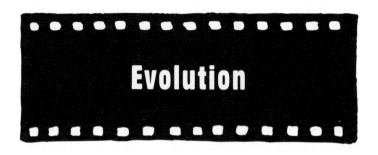

Evolution

. . . Harryhausen intended the film "to be the entire history of the planet." He said, "Naturally, I started with the dinosaurs because that's what interested me the most."

Yet another in our parade of nondirectorial auteurs, Ray Harryhausen is, technically speaking, an effects guy—a stop-motion animator. But his mastery of the craft carried him to the point where his productions could truly be called Ray Harryhausen films.

It's ironic that craftsmen of Harryhausen's sort tend to end up working in groups, because most of them started alone. In basements, barns, garages, and workshops, talented youngsters with a technical bent begin to cobble in private before sharing their gifts with the world. Ray Harryhausen was no exception, though his entry into the realm that brought him success came through a group—one of the first manifestations of organized fandom in the United States: the Los Angeles Science Fiction Society.

The Los Angeles Science Fiction Society met weekly during the early days of fandom in the 1930s. Clifton's Cafeteria in downtown Los Angeles was the venue where the clan gathered to celebrate their enthusiasm. The members included such promising youths as Ray Bradbury and Forrest J. Ackerman, and Harryhausen's association with such like-minded individuals led to the acquaintanceship that would launch his career.

As a teenager, Ray worked for George Pal on Puppetoons while simultaneously attending the University of Southern California—both group activities. After service in World War II (also a group activity), Ray returned to the solitary life of a solo artisan, crafting a series of short films based on the Mother Goose stories. They were similar to Pal's Puppetoons, but Harryhausen eschewed the multiple-head technique and wood-based construction that Pal had utilized, in favor of techniques he could implement himself.

So you see, Ray Harryhausen, today the object of so much fan enthusiasm, was just like so many of us—a fan. In some ways, he was like the characters derided in William Shatner's now-infamous "Get a Life" sketch from *Saturday Night Live*—a grown man, living at home, working on his models. (Harry's sole collaborators were his parents, who helped with the costumes and construction.) The only difference between Harryhausen and the majority of fans like him is that he just happened to be a talent of prodigious proportions.

Ray Harryhausen envisioned an animated film that would tell the entire history of the planet. It still lies dormant in his mind.

Harryhausen sold his 11-minute collection of Mother Goose films to an educational distributor, which marketed them to libraries and schools. They were so successful that Harryhausen made similar shorts well into the 1950s. Wisely, however, Harryhausen complemented his solitary activities with career-building forays into the world of big-time Hollywood entertainment.

He joined his hero, *King Kong* maestro Willis O'Brien, on O'Brien's nice-Kong movie, 1949's *Mighty Joe Young*. Harryhausen—essentially the successor to O'Brien as king of the stop-motion world—began to move up the professional ladder swiftly. He did stop-motion animation for *The Beast from 20,000 Fathoms*, *It Came from beneath the Sea*, and *Earth vs. the Flying Saucers*. With Obie (Willis O'Brien's nickname) he did a 15-minute prehistoric sequence for Irwin (*Poseidon Adventure*) Allen's 1956 *The Animal World*. Harryhausen worked on *20 Million Miles to Earth* and *The 27th Day*, adding to his collection of quintessential fifties sci-fi B movies. And in 1958 came the film that could be considered the foundation of all that

Harryhausen, the most prolific stop-motion animator ever, would never see his greatest vision completed.

would be known as "Ray Harryhausen movies"—*The 7th Voyage of Sinbad*.

He subsequently provided animation for films including *Mysterious Island* and *One Million Years B.C.* (no, he did not animate Raquel Welch!), but the rest of the true Harryhausen films are as follows: *Jason and the Argonauts* (1963), *First Men in the Moon* (1964), *The Valley of Gwangi* (1969) (it had been a pet project of his mentor, O'Brien), *The Golden Voyage of Sinbad* (1974), *Sinbad and the Eye of the Tiger* (1977), and *Clash of the Titans* (1981).

Harryhausen served as either co-producer or associate producer of these films, and on them he exerted an auteur's creative authority, to the point of writing some of the stories.

There are a number of Harryhausen projects that have gone un-realized, and at a certain point in the eighties Harryhausen basically realized that he had retired and that it wasn't worth wasting his life pursuing projects that wouldn't happen any time soon. Since then, he's made cameo appearances in a couple of films (*Beverly Hills Cop III* and *Spies like Us*) and has garnered awards and tributes. But new Harryhausen films are no more. It would be nice to be able to see the films he was working on during the eighties, but the most im-pressive unmade Harryhausen flick actually dates to the pre–World War II era of Harryhausen's solo work at home.

Young Harryhausen—by himself (except for Ma and Pa)—com-pleted a significant portion of a color stop-motion film titled *Evolu-tion*. According to reports, Harryhausen intended the film "to be the entire history of the planet." He said, "Naturally, I started with the dinosaurs because that's what interested me the most."

Harryhausen—to this day an avid collector of soundtracks—con-ceived the film with music in mind. For one sequence, he had been thinking of the *Firebird* Suite, "which has a certain chord in it that made [him] think, 'That's where an allosaurus should leap into frame!' "

That sequence is said to compare in detail and intricacy with Willis O'Brien's legendary *The Lost World*. Featured are glass paintings of gnarled trees and undergrowth and creepily hanging vegetation of one sort or another. Also painted is a mist through which a prehistoric giant marches as two birds made out of tin fly by on invisible wires. An allosaurus suddenly leaps into frame, causing the dinosaur to stagger backward.

This is the work of a true prodigy—a solo effort as intricate as a major studio release made more than a decade earlier, by a man who was simultaneously going to college and working for George Pal. Unfortunately, Harryhausen's enthusiasm dimmed when Walt Disney's *Fantasia* contained the similarly themed *Rites of Spring* segment. Then came the war and afterward Harryhausen stepped onto the path that made him.

He had intended to sell *Evolution* to the educational market, in which he was to have success with his later fairy tales. But it's the way Harryhausen has lived his life that's an education. Here is a guy who succeeded not only within the system but also alongside it, making films not just for money but also for love.

It's interesting to note that while we will never see the completed *Evolution*, young Ray had an experience making it that may well have made all subsequent Harryhausen pictures possible. One day, an agitated Ray bounced a hammer in frustration and accidentally destroyed a glass painting into which he had put lots of effort. He claimed that from that upsetting experience he learned to be patient.

That patience paid off in the form of a series of movies that will likely elicit cheers until the end of time.

1. A robot may not injure a human being or, through inaction, allow a human being to come to harm.

2. A robot must obey the orders given it by human beings except where such orders would conflict with the First Law.

3. A robot must protect its own existence so long as such protection does not conflict with the First or Second Laws.

These are known as the "Three Laws of Robotics," and they were written by noted sci-fi writer Isaac Asimov. They may seem like no great shakes to us because we've been to the movies and we've seen robots that are mean and hurtful—machine creatures of every shape and description. The "Three Laws of Robotics" are extremely significant, however, because they helped usher in the serious treatment of robotics in the literary and scientific worlds. If you are a fan of even the most accessible science fiction, such as the various *Star Trek* series, you have heard words and seen stories driven by notions conceived by Isaac Asimov.

Asimov, before his death in the early nineties, had written literally hundreds of books. As he was an actual scientist (he was a doctor of biochemistry), his books on science fact made otherwise difficult concepts accessible to the masses. A winner of the Nebula and Hugo awards, he managed to achieve both quality and quantity in his work.

Though listed as an adviser in the credits of *Star Trek: The Motion Picture* (don't blame him), this brilliant writer of novels and short stories, who influenced so much of what we've seen on screen, never wrote a film. In fact, none of his stories have ever been made into a movie. His authorship of the 1966 novelization of the film *Fantastic Voyage* may be the closest Asimov ever got to film success.

Yet Asimov stories call out for screen treatment. His *Caves of Steel* was described by reviewer Robert Irons as follows: "*The Caves of Steel* takes place on Earth. The fragile relationship between Earth and the 50 worlds colonized from Earth depends on New York detective Lije Baley's speedy solution of a murder case. Lije is partnered with investigator R. (for Robot) Daneel Olivaw. And Lije dislikes robots."

This was not familiar stuff in 1953. No *Alien Nation* had established the sort of partnership that is described here. So much that we take for granted began with Asimov and was then taken up by others.

Asimov himself had a few major brushes with Hollywood. In the late eighties, he was approached by producers who were interested in doing a sequel to *Fantastic Voyage*. Since he had written the novelization, they decided he should write a new novel, which would then be transferred to film.

The Hollywood types told Asimov exactly what they wanted him to "write." The original *Fantastic Voyage* had been about miniaturized humans traveling through a person's bloodstream in a sort of submarine. The producers behind the sequel wanted two submarines—one American, the other Soviet. According to Asimov, they were looking for World War III in the bloodstream. Asimov believed that the United States and Russia would not be adversarial in the future and (because of this and other disagreements) did not accept the assignment.

Subsequently, another scribe took on the challenge and gave the producers exactly what they wanted. (Asimov thought the other writer's work was terrific.) Of course, the producers were unhappy with it and came back to Asimov, who wrote a more complex and idealistic version, which was a failure. The movie was never made. To his death, Asimov believed the project would have been a success if his sponsors had used the other guy's work.

Asimov was like other fine writers whose works were not containable enough for Hollywood. He took advantage of the unlimited canvas offered by the written word and could not waste time being constrained by Hollywood's "rules." Polish interviewer Slawek Wojtowicz asked Asimov, "Have you ever written any screenplays for SF movies?" Asimov replied, "No, I've no talent for that and I don't want to get mixed up with Hollywood. If they are going to do something of mine, they will have to find someone else to write the screenplays."

This is not atypical among novelists. Many don't care whether they write their own movies because the movie is not the point. It's just an ancillary item, like the toys in a Happy Meal. The work is already done—it's all in the book.

In the 1970s, however, a novelist who did write for Hollywood (despite his constant complaints) was entrusted with the task of adapting Asimov's *I, Robot* for the screen. Asimov believed Harlan Ellison's script would have made "the first really adult, complex, worthwhile science fiction movie." Typically the screenplay was serialized in a magazine and published in book form but never made it to the screen.

Meanwhile, just a few years later, others were trying to adapt Asimov's *Foundation* for the screen. The original *Foundation* trilogy stands alongside Asimov's robot stories as his most important work in the field of science fiction. (The author eventually connected the two series.)

The *Foundation* novels comprise an epic survey of future history and would be more likely to support a series of pictures than a single epic. This was not too long after the Salkinds made multiple Musketeer and Superman pictures simultaneously, and producer Michael

Phillips determined that he was going to take on not one but all three of the original *Foundation* novels.

Asimov told Slawek Wojtowicz, "Oh, every once in a while somebody talks about doing [*Foundation*], but so far nobody has ever managed to dig up enough money for it."

Michael Phillips had split from his wife, Julia, with whom he had co-produced *Close Encounters of the Third Kind,* and while she tumbled into drug-induced failure he failed by making pictures like the robot comedy *Heartbeeps.* He went so far as to hire director David Ward for the *Foundation* project, but Phillips, stung by a string of failures, couldn't raise the money to keep the project going. When he realized he could go no further, he announced, "I've loved these books since college and someday, at a more opportune moment in terms of financing, I'd like to make them as films."

Flash-forward to 1994, when—two years after Asimov's death—TriStar Pictures decided it was an opportune moment for them to dig up some money and purchase the rights to *Foundation.* TriStar spent two productive years not producing a picture until the rights were sold again, this time to New Line, in 1996.

New Line took the bull by the horns and assigned *Species* screenwriter Dennis Feldman to work on a script. He would cover just the first novel—*Foundation*—in which future citizen Hari Seldon discovers that humanity will inevitably return to its previous state of barbarity. Feldman promised to include as much of the content and spirit of the book as he could. As of this writing, *Foundation* is not on New Line's release slate.

Some notions just seem too big for the limited scope of the Hollywood movie. But when Hollywood figures out how to tackle the really big ideas, movies will have taken that long-delayed next step in their development as a literary form. In the meantime, while we may not see a filmed adaptation of Isaac Asimov's *Foundation,* we can take comfort in the fact that his ideas have provided a foundation for so much of the science fiction we have already seen.

Francis Ford Coppola's Pinocchio

"He's a bad-boy Pinocchio," said Coppola . . .

Film artists tend to have relationships with specific studios. They find people with whom they feel comfortable and tend to work with them again and again. So, when an executive moves to a new locale, many relationships move right along with him. Woody Allen, for instance, moved from his longtime home at United Artists to Orion Pictures when the men who ran UA founded the latter firm.

Conversely, there are people and places some filmmakers dare not involve themselves with. What may be a congenial home for Director A might turn out to be a snake pit from the perspective of Director B.

Warner Bros., for example, was the longtime home of director Stanley Kubrick. Kubrick picked his own projects, took as long as he wanted to make them, and delivered them to the studio when he was good and ready. From a filmmaker's perspective, that made Warner Bros. a happy home indeed.

But to Francis Ford Coppola—like Kubrick one of the great directors of the modern era—Warner Bros. is not a happy home. Rather, it's a recurring nightmare, a repository of bad memories and professional dangers.

It's not as if Warners didn't play a significant role in Coppola's rise to success. Though his greatest hits have been Paramount's *Godfather* pictures (and his recent successes have been at Columbia), Coppola's first relationship with a major studio was actually with Warner Bros.

When young Coppola worked his way out of the exploitation and Corman environs wherein he had apprenticed, he was a rising talent in the Seven Arts production concern. Seven Arts gave Coppola his first opportunity to direct a real Hollywood movie, and the result was the critically lauded coming-of-age comedy *You're a Big Boy Now.*

By the time *You're a Big Boy Now* was released, Seven Arts had acquired Warner Bros. (renamed Warner Bros.–Seven Arts) and Coppola was a comer within the organization. He was given a prize project, the Fred Astaire starrer, *Finian's Rainbow,* and, despite the fact that it was a flop, also given financial support to start his own company, American Zoetrope.

Within a couple of years, however, Seven Arts had unloaded Warner Bros. to a company called Kinney National Service (renamed Warner Communications). Meanwhile, American Zoetrope had produced two unsuccessful films—George Lucas's *THX-1138* and Coppola's *The Rain People.* Warners demanded the return of money it had given Coppola, who had used it to equip his beloved Zoetrope. The result was Coppola's tumble into one of his many financial reverses. (But the upside was he was available as a director-for-hire when *The Godfather* came around.)

It's the relationship thing. Coppola had positive relationships at the Warners run by Seven Arts but did not have a happy relationship with his masters over at Warner Communications. Conversely, though a long-gone Columbia regime failed with *One from the Heart,* in more recent years, a top executive there has been former Zoetrope exec Lucy Fisher. Modern Columbia is, therefore, a congenial home for him.

Unlike Columbia, Warner Bros. has had a relatively stable management for decades, which is good for Kubrick, bad for Coppola. That's why Coppola was not enthusiastic about going back when encouraged to develop projects there in the early nineties. Nevertheless, there were things Coppola wanted to do, so he proceeded . . . cautiously. Ultimately, he was saddened but unsurprised when the studio remained an uncongenial home for him.

Unfortunately, one of the things Coppola put into development while at Warners was a project that was dear to him—a live-action/ animation/puppet production of *Pinocchio*.

Now, everyone knows that Francis Ford Coppola is a great film artist. Everyone also knows that financial reversals brought on by the scope of his ambitions have caused him to lose his footing. Even his successes during most of the eighties and nineties have been compromises of one sort or another, the work of a man trying to find his way back to solid ground. But there are things for which the master still has passion, and if he were able to pursue those things, free of worries and encumbrances, he would be Francis Ford Coppola again.

Coppola has always had passion for his family. (His foolhardy use of daughter Sofia in *The Godfather, Part III* was the most public expression of his familial orientation.) As an expansive, emotional Italian family man, Coppola never had a worse experience than when he lost his son in a boating accident while making *Gardens of Stone*. That's why Coppola's *Pinocchio* was such an extraordinary project. Coppola saw the film as the story of a father who lost his son. The film was to be his own story.

And it was a story that led him to Brian Henson at Jim Henson Productions. Henson was to handle puppet work for the movie, and the project would prove meaningful to him, too. He saw *Pinocchio* as the story of a boy who had lost his father. Having recently lost his dad, Jim Henson, Brian felt Coppola's *Pinocchio* was his story as well.

So the personal and artistic passions of two prodigiously talented family men were funneled into a project that would speak to us all. It wasn't a gangster movie like *The Godfather* or a horror movie like Coppola's version of *Dracula* or a Muppet movie made for kids. This was Pinocchio. This was for everyone.

But Warner Bros. didn't want to do it, so Coppola took the project to Columbia, which was genuinely interested. Unfortunately, when

Columbia expressed its interest Warner Bros. suddenly claimed the project was theirs.

Coppola felt Warner Bros. "had no respect" for him. He said the project was his idea to begin with and that he had personally paid artists to do storyboards, written multiple drafts of the script, and even composed its songs. When negotiations with Warners got difficult, he had assured the studio that he would personally take on much of the financial burden of producing the film, as he had done many times before. But it was to no avail.

Warner Bros.' insistence on its ownership rights killed the deal at Columbia. Courtroom battles resulted and Coppola now feels the movie will never be made. (For one thing, a version starring Martin Landau has been made since Coppola's project fell through.) That means audiences will never get to see the costume designs that Chanel's Karl Lagerfeld had agreed to provide for actors such as Christopher Walken, Anthony Quinn, and Lauren Bacall or the Pinocchio puppet that stood three and one-half feet tall.

Coppola had tested a number of animation techniques for the film, but his favorite was the classic stop-motion approach. "He's a bad-boy Pinocchio," said Coppola, sounding like a child as he discussed the puppet that represented the child he had lost. And now he'd lost this one as well.

Good Girls

I think it's too weird, which is exactly why it should be made.

Hollywood doesn't like freaks. Oh, sure, there have been all sorts of freakish characters, but they're almost always treated like . . . well, freaks. Tod Browning's controversial cult-classic *Freaks* shocked audiences upon its release in 1932. Featuring a cast of real-life freaks bent on revenge on their abusive circus taskmasters, the film was repeatedly banned and kept out of distribution for thirty years. The film nearly ruined director Browning's career. Even David Lynch's *Elephant Man*, though presented as a sympathetic character, leads an extraordinary life—a freakish one. His plight need not intrude too strongly upon the audience's own sense of reality.

But real freaks walk the earth with us every day. Extra fingers, webbed toes, strange garb, odd ways of being. Hell, a lot of us *are* freaks, and we walk the earth with the normal folk every day. We might as well have three breasts for all the integration we feel with the society around us.

Artists—freaks every one of 'em—can take the sense of not belonging and transmute it via iconography into something recognizable and metaphoric. Tim Burton, with *Edward Scissorhands,* presented his own outsider's stance in the form of the oddly digited character's relationship with the world. But *Edward Scissorhands* was about a lone outsider in a world of normals. In this regard, it was really just another *Elephant Man*. It was left to Carol Lay, in her comic strip *Good Girls,* to give us a world that is full of freaks, though still defined by the normals. The world of the *Good Girls* cartoon, exaggeration aside, is the world we live in.

Good Girls is the story of Irene Van de Kamp, an heiress who grew up in "darkest" Africa after her parents were killed while traveling there. She is raised as a "Bongodian" and, when ultimately returned to her rightful life and position in America, is regarded as hideous because of the African disk in her elongated lower lip. She is indulged because of her wealth, but her sensitivity allow her to see the truth, so she is an outsider . . . alone.

Lay came up with the idea for *Good Girls* when

Good Girls is a romantic comic book that was turned into a script. This offbeat romance is still in search of a studio with an open mind.

I had a fight with my then-boyfriend which broke my heart a little. I had just read a DC Comics collection of romance comics called Heart Throbs, *so I got into a soapy kind of mood. The story I liked the best in there was the only one that had a sad, realistic ending. I had also recently seen a picture of three Ubangi-type women in a* Hustler *magazine that this same boyfriend showed me. So, instead of moping about or being angry, I put the hideous face together with the soapy romance style and wrote a ten page comic story about Irene Van de Kamp, Bongodian heiress. She's rich, she's sweet, and she's got a face only an anthropologist could love. Problem is, she falls in love with a lawyer.*

Irene Van de Camp was simply a girl on a quest for true love.

Lay continued: "I wrote and drew the comic sometime in 1980. It first appeared in a SubGenius rag called *The Stark Fist of Removal.* In 1984 or so I put together the first of my *Good Girls* comics and used it there. Fantagraphics Books did the first 5 issues."

The strip was successful by comic standards—at least for a while: "The first issue sold 15,000 copies, but then the black-and-white comics market crashed. The rest sold out, but the print runs were small. Fantagraphics did not actively promote the book so I went to Rip Off, but by then the market was bad for everybody. It had a loyal cult following, which is what I expected."

Members of the cult soon encouraged a film adaptation. Jerry Casale of Devo, together with Roman Coppola, wanted to utilize the character. Unfortunately, says Lay, "I was too naive to help it along." Ultimately, a picture was developed with a B-movie producer named Matt Devlin, and while nothing resulted in the way of an actual film, Lay produced a screenplay that was an affecting mixture of pulp, comic, film, and literary ideas.

We've often heard of women having faces that only blind men could love, but Irene has a face not even a blind man can love. Her protruding lip is repulsive even to the touch, as her blind boyfriend discovers. Irene's cinematic adventure takes her to an island of "freaks," including a two-headed man and a woman so fat that bullets get lost in her flab. But these freaks were to the manner born. Irene, on the other hand, is a freak in the normal world and a normal in freaksville. Regardless, her soul is so beautiful that she is willing to sacrifice her own happiness for higher callings. But don't get the idea that *Good Girls* is sappy. In the screenplay, she is hunted down for business reasons by her own uncle and the story mixes comedy, adventure, romance, and cartoon oddity in equal measure.

This sort of thing is not weird when encountered within the pages of a comic book. Comic fans

Good Girls's heartwarming story did not seem to touch movie-studio executives who couldn't get over the lead character's beautifully disfigured features. That's Hollywood.

expect storytelling that uses a more stylized visual lexicon. But when stories like this are transferred to film, the intrinsic "reality" of film renders them jarring and impactful. That makes *Good Girls* potentially better on film than in print. What is film if not a medium in which worlds can be created? We ought to be creating some better worlds. And when we do, audiences will sit up and take notice.

Lay understands Hollywood's timidity, saying of her script, "I think it's too weird, which is exactly why it should be made. The first time it fell through was my doing, but I can only imagine why no one picked it up after that. My theory is that conventionally minded men run the show and these kinds of men don't get why Irene is fabulous. If a woman looks like anything other than a Playmate, they don't want to look at her. Irene's face is extreme."

This touching tale can still be enjoyed as a six-issue series of romance comics.

Sounds a bit like life imitating art. Male executives react to Irene the way the characters in the comic do—which points to the essential truth of the material.

Good Girls is, at heart, a tragi-comic romance, which we so often experience in life. It just happens to feature a lead character who has "a lip disk, a nose plug, scarification, and a duck-tailed haircut.

"The beauty theme that runs through it is always timely," says Lay, "but maybe it would help if she would explode. Guys like that."

Carol, don't change a thing.

Harrow Alley

... George C. Scott purchased the property, which he has owned into the nineties. ... "I can always get the financing if I allow them to fuck it up, you see, but that I won't allow."

Harrow Alley is widely regarded as one of the finest unproduced screenplays in circulation. Though written by Walter Brown Newman, whose movies include *Cat Ballou* and *The Man with the Golden Arm* (and—uncredited—*The Great Escape* and *The Magnificent Seven*), I approached it with skepticism and trepidation. Battle-scarred by previous entanglements with the overhyped, I feared the piece would be unable to match my expectations. Imagine my surprise when it actually turned out to be an astonishing piece of work—a work of entertainment and instruction, an unflinching document of the human condition, and the blueprint for one hell of a movie. The script is about what happens when *Harrow Alley* a middle-class community in seventeenth-century London, is hit by the bubonic plague. The enclave of busy stores and street merchants hopes it can escape the disease that has hit so many other communities. Inexorably, however, little by little, death becomes the dominant figure in the life of the parish.

The piece begins with a convict named Ratsey about to be executed by the local hangman. Unexpectedly, the hangman's apprentice succumbs to the plague and Ratsey's life is spared. He becomes a ward of Harry Poyntz, a prosperous tailor and alderman of London's Harrow Alley area, and is assigned the task of handling the dead bodies resulting from the plague. Ratsey feels like the luckiest man in the world, since he survived the plague as a child and is sure he can't get it again.

When Harry first brings Ratsey to Harrow Alley, the community is strong. Business is good, friendships thrive, life shows tremendous promise, and Alderman Poyntz is about to become a father. In short order, various pillars of the community, including the king himself, flee London to avoid the infirmity. It is left to those who remain behind to maintain a sense of continuity in the community, to maintain the community itself until normalcy can return.

There are elements of the script that are reminiscent of *High Noon*. In the face of great fear, many back down and flee, leaving only a few to carry on in behalf of their weak brethren. Unlike *High Noon*, however, in which Gary Cooper's character is a "hero" to the end, no one in Harrow Alley remains unchanged.

Harry, worried about his unborn child's prospects for survival, wants to join the fleeing mob, but the mayor of London tells him that only the continued presence of important men such as themselves will comfort the public and allow civic life to go on. Harry tells the mayor that there is no punishment that would keep him from leaving to protect his family. The mayor replies that Harry will stay, nonetheless, because he is good. Harry, knowing the mayor is correct, feels that he has been damned.

And damned he has been. At one point, Harry sees grass growing up through the cobblestones and fears that the neighborhood is disappearing. But it's Harry who disappears. Try though he might, he does not save the day. Though he is our protagonist through most of the picture, his inability to control the havoc, combined with the unexpected revelation that his wife's new child is not his own, ultimately breaks him. He disappears from the story some three-quarters of the way into the show, but the story goes on, just like life itself. Harrow Alley itself is the star of the show. People may come and go, but the community remains.

On the street, we meet courageous men like the baker who remains in town because the people have to have bread. We see weaklings like the prosperous man who locks himself and his family inside the house for the duration. When his tiny son sneaks out, the fearful man—believing he is protecting the rest of his brood—does not let him back in.

There is the black Jamaican, Toby, who is forced to help with the corpses, the mute who takes in orphaned children, the aged doctor who sacrifices his own life to explore the innards of a plague victim. This mix of characters and their contrasting reactions under duress is reminiscent of some *Twilight Zone* episodes wherein human character is put to the test in the face of a nuclear disaster or some similar crisis. *Harrow Alley,* however, addresses these inner and outer conflicts on an epic scale.

Ratsey, who comports himself fairly honorably throughout the crisis, is pardoned by Harry before the alderman disappears. Eventually, Ratsey marries the baker's widow and becomes a baker himself and a part-time constable for the community. It is in this capacity that he arrests a disheveled fellow who stabbed two associates because their bickering annoyed him.

Ratsey recognizes the soul-deadened murderer as Harry Poyntz, the man who once pardoned him. But this is no story about a grateful lion who once had a thorn removed from his paw. This is real life. The movie ends when Ratsey deposits Harry in the very prison from which he had rescued Ratsey.

When *Harrow Alley* was written during the early 1960s, John Huston wanted to direct it, but a couple of flops rendered him temporarily unbankable. Producer Ingo Preminger optioned it after Huston's option expired, and in 1968 George C. Scott purchased the property, which he has owned into the nineties. Scott had been associated with the project since the Huston days, when there had been talk of Peter O'Toole as Harry and Scott as Ratsey.

As recently as 1988, production seemed more or less imminent. At that time, David Hemmings was to direct, with a cast including Trish Van Devere, Martin Sheen, and Brian Dennehy. George C. Scott was to play the aging Dr. Hodges.

Scott told an interviewer, "We couldn't get the financing; it's as simple as that." He went on to say, "I can always get the financing if I allow them to fuck it up, you see, but that I won't allow."

Even more recently, a deal with the Hungarian film authorities was nearly set but collapsed. In a way, it seems, the script is too great to be produced. Says Scott, "Whoever's interested in financing it seems to want to cut it, and I have insisted, since I purchased it in 1968, that it not be cut." Maintaining the integrity of this great script seems to mean maintaining it in script form only.

Scott continues to keep the faith. ". . . this is a kind of insurance policy, this script," he asserts. He has lately considered Mel Gibson for the role of Harry and Kenneth Branagh for the role of Ratsey. "Yes!" Scott has stated. "It's kept me alive all these years. I'm very serious, and when it gets done, my work is done. That's how strongly I feel about it."

Heart of Darkness

Ladies and gentlemen, this is Orson Welles. Don't worry; there's just nothing to look at for a while. You can close your eyes if you want to, but . . . please open them when I tell you to.

Everybody knows that Orson Welles came to Hollywood at the age of twenty-five and made *Citizen Kane*, which was an artistic triumph and set in motion a series of events that had repercussions for the remainder of the director's career. What most people don't know, however, is that when radio and theater titan Welles arrived in California *Citizen Kane* was not the picture he intended to make.

"In the course of signing the deal, it was agreed that it would be *Heart of Darkness*. It was a direct result of radio—and we'd done *Heart of Darkness* on the radio. I came to Hollywood and wrote the script." So said Welles many years after the start of his troubled Hollywood career. Welles's career was to be filled with projects that never came to fruition, but the pattern was set with his intended production of this Joseph Conrad novel.

Heart of Darkness is the classic story of Marlow and his trek up a jungle river to find and kill Kurtz, a trader who became a jungle natives' god. Welles intended the story as an attack on fascism. In a

Before *Citizen Kane*, Orson Welles had planned to make *Hearts of Darkness*. Parts of the film would be seen entirely in the first person.

memo, Welles wrote: "The picture is, frankly, an attack on the Nazi system."

Marlow was to be a representative of an unnamed foreign government. In the words of a contemporaneous studio memo, the picture was to have had "cannibals, shooting, petty bickering among the bureaucrats, native dances . . . There is a jungle in flames and heavy storms of a spectacular nature . . ."

As he had on radio, Welles was to play both Marlow (the narrator) and Kurtz. (He later claimed that at the last minute he abandoned the notion of playing Kurtz.) The picture was to have been shot from the perspective of Marlow—Marlow was to have been the camera. The audience would see his reflection in the glass of the pilot's compartment in the paddle steamer; they would see his hand as he lit his cigarette. In short, they would see only what would be visible if they themselves were Marlow.

The opening was to have been a black screen, as Welles began the narration:

"Ladies and gentlemen, this is Orson Welles. Don't worry; there's just nothing to look at for a while. You can close your eyes if you want to, but . . . please open them when I tell you to.

"Everything you see is going to be seen through your eyes and you're somebody else."

The audience was to have been placed in the position of a murderer about to be put to death in the electric chair, followed by other first-person sequences. Then the unseen Marlow was to light a ciga-rette and the real story of the picture was to begin.

This playful series of first-person "demonstrations" was, of course, classic Welles. He loved to play with his audiences, with his media, as was evident in his theatrical work, his radio work, and, of course, his film work, from day one to the bitter end. (Witness the whimsy in his last completed picture, 1976's *F for Fake.*) The series of dem-onstrations was clearly from the same artist/entertainer who had been responsible for the faux newscast structure of radio's *War of the Worlds.*

And while the young Welles had produced many innovative tri-umphs in the theater, he was nationally known through his radio appearances, particularly *War of the Worlds.* Frightening a nation into believing they've been attacked by Martians is liable to give you a great deal of notoriety, and it certainly did in Welles's case. It was reported that the RKO board would have preferred that Welles make *War of the Worlds* as his first film, but RKO production head George Schaefer wanted prestige and even controversy from Welles and was willing to let him have his way. (Much is made of the preponderance of research that now goes into the development of American enter-tainment, but as far back as 1939, when Welles began his Hollywood career, RKO commissioned a Gallup poll to see what audiences wanted Welles to make. It is to Schaefer's credit that he let Welles attempt *Heart of Darkness,* which was among those least desired by those polled.)

Intense preparation went into the film. Welles later claimed it was the most preparation any of his films ever had. Models of the sets were built, and Welles did a day of test shooting that included use of the virtually unheard-of hand-held camera technique. The cast had signed their contracts. (Many were unknowns, but among them was Norman Lloyd, later an associate of Alfred Hitchcock and still later Dr. Auschlander on television's *St. Elsewhere.*)

Unfortunately, as the antifascist piece was being prepared Hitler invaded Poland and the beginning of World War II helped spell the end of Welles's plans. The loss of the European box office meant budgets had to be tighter. And *Heart of Darkness*'s budget had already been assessed at something like twice the $500,000 that had been allotted for it.

Welles had been ready to pour his typically encompassing artistic passion into the effort. He had toured the RKO tech shops and learned everything he could about the magic of film. He intended to use techniques that would not become commonplace for decades. Even his sense of character was unbridled in comparison to the general approaches of the Hollywood machine. He had, for instance, intended to portray Marlow as a man of uncontrollable passion—a man who couldn't keep his hands off his woman.

Still, we probably shouldn't be sad, since Welles's passions were rechanneled into *Citizen Kane*, which many believe to be the greatest picture ever made. After all, every time you do one thing there are many other things left undone. *Heart of Darkness* is the great picture Orson Welles might have made; *Citizen Kane* is the great picture he made.

But, interestingly, before proceeding with Kane, there was yet another picture Orson Welles almost made but didn't. It was to have been called *The Smiler with a Knife,* and for the female lead Welles had wanted a young Lucille Ball. What would her life and career have been like if that had happened? (Francis Ford Coppola later based *Apocalypse Now* on *Heart of Darkness.* If Welles had made his film, perhaps Coppola would never have made his!)

And what would have happened to Welles if he had been able to make *Heart of Darkness* instead of *Citizen Kane*? Perhaps he would never have made an enemy of newspaper magnate William Randolph Hearst, on whom Kane was partially based. Maybe Welles's career would have gone more smoothly and been filled with more opportunity. But we'll never know.

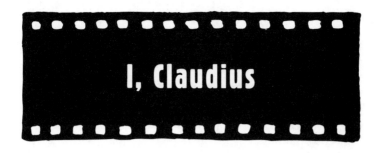

I, Claudius

. . . Laughton's work (as seen in the surviving footage) has been called "one of the greatest performances in the history of the cinema."

Josef von Sternberg, the director who added the *von* to his name for added directorial impact, the director who grew up in America but made a name for himself in Germany, was one of the great visual stylists of the motion picture screen. His films are chockablock with textbook examples of how to layer a shot with foreground and background. He painted images with light and shadow and smoke and substance in a series of films that have stood the test of time. Most of these films were with Marlene Dietrich, who had been both his star and his lover. In 1936, both relationships were in the past.

Charles Laughton was a great English actor who believed that acting was as important as any of the arts and should be approached as such. He wanted to be as great as the greatest poets and sculptors and painters. Many believe that he achieved this goal.

Alexander Korda was a motion picture producer in England. In 1936, he was in the midst of a love affair with actress Merle Oberon. Some have said it was necessary for Korda to further Oberon's career in order to hold onto her.

All these people's various life stories converged on the ill-fated

Charles Laughton from Cecil B. DeMille's *The Sign of the Cross*. He was dressed similarly for his role in the doomed production of *I, Claudius*.

1936 production of *I, Claudius,* based on the novel by Robert Graves concerning the life of Tiberius Claudius Drusus Nero Germanicus (10 B.C.–A.D. 54). Looked upon as an idiot because of his infirmities and deformities, Claudius managed to survive the murderous, duplicitous regimes of Augustus, Tiberius, and Caligula to become emperor of Rome in A.D. 41. The picture was to show the many indignities the man had to suffer based solely on his appearance. In some ways (though not in degree of physical oddity), the story is reminiscent of *The Elephant Man.* Claudius was not an animal—he was a human being—but people couldn't or wouldn't see it. (If there is any question as to whether Laughton was appropriate for such a role, one need only remember that this is a man who movingly portrayed the Hunchback of Notre Dame.)

Alexander Korda's original choice to direct *I, Claudius* had been William Cameron Menzies, who had directed the H. G. Wells classic *Things to Come* (and would go on to make a definitive contribution to *Gone with the Wind*). Von Sternberg got the job because Marlene Dietrich insisted Korda take on the director if he could not pay her $100,000 he owed her. However, since Dietrich asserted that von Sternberg could do for Merle Oberon what he had done for Dietrich herself, Korda stood to reap extra benefits from the choice.

Unfortunately, this was not a good time in von Sternberg's life.

Fed up with Hollywood, he built himself an isolated home in the desert, only to decide it was not isolated enough. He embarked upon a trip to the Far East to get farther away but at some point, due to problems emotional and/or physical, ended up in a London hospital. This was where Korda was to find him. Once signed for the film, however, von Sternberg was himself again, even wearing to the set a turban he had acquired in his travels.

Von Sternberg believed filmmaking to be "an interplay of light and shadow, of foreground and background, point and counterpoint, inclusion and exclusion of content, a balance of pictorial and acoustic impact." He believed that "an actor is rewarded with attention out of proportion to his services." He also wrote: "An actor is turned on and off like a spigot, and like the spigot, is not the source of the liquid that flows through him."

This was not likely to be an approach conducive to working with a sensitive actor like Laughton. Laughton wanted to explore the character in detail with a director who was "opposed to no method [Laughton] might think valid for impersonating himself."

Laughton had previously been treated kindly by the director on a personal basis and did not openly defy him. But the director's indifference to the actor's craft played upon Laughton's insecurities. The footage that exists shows Laughton stopping in the middle of seemingly perfect takes and damning one or another aspect of his work. And yet Laughton's work (as seen in the surviving footage) has been called "one of the greatest performances in the history of the cinema." It is a performance of startling breadth, depth, and sensitivity. Laughton's expressions as he walked through a jeering, hateful mob could convey to an idiot the definition of pathos. Von Sternberg had wanted "to show how a nobody became a god, and became a nobody and nothing again" and through Laughton's performance would have been able to achieve his goals.

But the sensitive Laughton, though in touch with his thespian greatness, was unable to work with a director who gave him nothing. And von Sternberg was unwilling and/or unable to shed his indifferent approach to the actor's needs. So Laughton ended giving one of the great performances of his career while falling apart emotionally.

Suddenly another reality intruded upon the proceedings. Leading lady Merle Oberon was involved in a car accident, and production had to be shut down. Korda tried to get Claudette Colbert to replace Oberon, but Colbert wasn't interested. And so ended the story of the Korda/von Sternberg/Laughton production of *I, Claudius*.

It turns out, however, that Oberon wasn't very seriously injured in the crash. It's just that by this time von Sternberg was ensconced in a British mental hospital. It seems Laughton was not the only one buckling under the pressure. Indeed, Laughton might have been able to finish the film. But von Sternberg, unable to bend, was more than able to break. Some accounts have portrayed Laughton as a gibbering prima donna responsible for the production's collapse. But the existing footage from *I, Claudius* shows a greatness (albeit of a different kind)that belies the self-serving assertions of those who stood to gain from putting Laughton down. The surviving footage from *I, Claudius* can be found in a documentary titled *The Epic That Never Was*. Indeed.

I Loved a Soldier

In its way, Marlene Dietrich's transformation was to have been the glamour equivalent of Dr. Jekyll's transformation into Mr. Hyde.

One of the grand and glorious effects of the old Hollywood studio system was that movies could be made for a variety of reasons not available today. At a time when screenwriters and directors squabble publicly over who is really the "author" of a film, the fragile notions upon which films were hung fifty, sixty, and seventy years ago seem quite inconceivable. (Of course our era is possessed of fragile notions of its own.) Though we look back now and see the glories of what we call Frank Capra films and John Ford films, and though these men were famous in their day, movies during Hollywood's studio era were—in the minds of the public—about fundamentally different things than they are today.

One of the things that movies were about in those halcyon days was simply "the movies." In a pretelevision era, people went to their neighborhood theater on a regular basis to see whatever was to be seen—in much the same way that we now flick a switch to "see what's on TV." The freedom that regular attendance gave filmmakers was extraordinary. To a great extent, people would see their movie, no

matter what it was, so the filmakers had license to be bad if they so desired, but they also had license to be glorious—a certain amount of money would be made under any circumstances.

Further benefiting the studios was their ownership of key theaters throughout the United States and the fact that they booked "programs" of films into theaters. (They didn't sell each feature individually to exhibitors.) Thus they had guaranteed distribution for any picture they chose to make. (This also facilitated the production of live-action and cartoon shorts, which can be less economically feasible when you have to sell your items individually.) This foundation of freedom was largely responsible for the difference between the kinds of pictures we got then and the kinds of pictures we get now. A film like the most recent *Godzilla*—widely condemned for its lack of story value—is in many ways the result of the piecemeal film-buying system we have today. Because films are no longer sold in bulk and because studios cannot legally utilize "blind bidding" (whereby films are sold to theaters sight unseen, often before they are made), footage must be shown to theater owners before they will agree to lease them. In this environment, incomplete films that demonstrate impressive visual effects can seem mighty compelling to a theater owner. As a result (in conjunction with the "blockbuster mentality" that has prevailed for other reasons) theater owners and audiences sometimes end up with a picture whose sole value is the spectacle via which it was sold.

One of the likely reasons for the recent success of so-called independent films is that they were made first and marketed later. They were completed, generally speaking, for their value as films and then exhibited based on their actual quality. In the newest "New Hollywood," this might be the only way to ensure a flow of good films. In "Old Hollywood," a supply of good films flowed for the opposite reason. Old Hollywood didn't have

Marlene Dietrich's planned comeback never saw the light of day.

to show anything to anyone. It could make what it wanted. This system enabled the studios to keep on staff a large contingent of theatrical artisans plus a full stable of stars.

Today a star serves as a means of getting financing—to a real extent, he or she is just another special effect. Stars are "created" accidentally and then exploited in order to successfully "open" bad films, and when they've appeared in enough bad films and their credibility is destroyed they are replaced by newer accidentally created stars. In contrast, Old Hollywood actually created stars. As a consequence of the system I described earlier, studios could take as long as they wanted to develop actors and, once they did, these actors were carefully nurtured and maintained. Films, therefore, could be carefully crafted solely to best display the gifts of the treasured stars.

During the 1930s, one of Paramount's most treasured stars was Marlene Dietrich. Through a series of films directed by the great visual stylist Josef von Sternberg, Dietrich had become an exotic European ideal in the hearts and minds of the American public. Sometimes, however, a star's "personality" could become a prison. Even when handled by the studio with the utmost care, a star could

fall out of fashion with the public; his or her shtick could become tiresome.

Katherine Hepburn, after her early success, became so unpopular that she was labeled "box office poison." Her comeback vehicle, *The Philadelphia Story* (written with her involvement), was designed to humanize her, focusing on her "unapproachable" qualities and then knocking her down a peg and showing her to be "a good sport." She emerged from this reintroduction to become one of the great stars of all time. Dietrich, after her string of von Sternberg films, was thought to be in need of a similar humanization. The great director Ernst Lubitsch, who was in charge of production for Paramount at that time, was determined to oversee the necessary transformation himself.

The first picture to come out of the Dietrich humanization program was the Dietrich/Gary Cooper *Desire,* and its success prompted Lubitsch to to take the process a step further. A film was crafted based solely on the notion of a Dietrich "transformation." The audience would see just how an ordinary woman becomes a goddess like Marlene Dietrich. The secret, of course, is love.

"It is not a bad idea this [director] Henry Hathaway has," opined Dietrich. ". . . Not a bad idea to let love transform her in front of the camera."

"Making the transition, that's easy," felt the German-born star. "First we do no false lashes, use only a light brown mascara on my own; do a thin mouth, powdered down. Leave off the nose line but shadow the sides. Set the key light lower—make a baby face. Also, no inside white line on the eyes, so they will be very round. Then, we slowly add . . . First the mouth fuller, then the nose thinner, then very slowly, we bring the mystery into the eyes, move the key light higher for each take until we have . . . Dietrich." (There are even directors today who don't have Dietrich's degree of technical understanding!)

The story that was chosen to serve as a vehicle for the transformation had been used before. It had been a play and a silent movie and would later form the basis of Billy Wilder's *Five Graves to Cairo*. But the story was not the point; this film was to be about the transformation. Henry Hathaway, a former von Sternberg associate who was to have directed the picture under Lubitsch's supervision, described his vision of the transformation:

> *My idea for* Hotel Imperial *[the original title] was to start with a shot of a long, wide hallway, and a woman scrubbing and mopping the floor. She has dirty hair and dirty clothes, she is wearing old carpet slippers. She's a slob. As she gets [Charles Boyer] and . . . falls in love with him, she gets progressively prettier. Then you see Dietrich in all her beauty coming out of the cathedral married, with the Uhlan swordsmen framing her on either side. She has become completely transformed.*

Only in the Hollywood of yesteryear could an entire film be hung on such a transformation. Yet anyone who has seen the great Dietrich classics knows that her allure, supported by the visuals of Hollywood's master artisans, is reason enough to see a film—and see it again and again. In a film such as this, the scenario is necessary only to give audiences a chance to enjoy the star's beauty, just as stories were relatively incidental to Hollywood musicals, which were designed to showcase singing and dancing. (Still, unlike today, competent story construction was usually employed rather than ignored.) In its way, Dietrich's transformation was to have been the glamour equivalent of Dr. Jekyll's transformation into Mr. Hyde. The mysteries of monsters and sex goddesses are equally fascinating, and you can count on audiences to be interested in an entertainment that shows them the link between ordinary citizens and these otherworldly creatures.

Of course, Dietrich, despite her understanding of the role, allowed some star vanity to come into play during the production of *I Married a Soldier* (as the film was ultimately called). She would come to the set looking somewhat better than was intended for the scene at hand. "You're not supposed to be beautiful until next Thursday," Hathaway once scolded. "Please, can't it at least be Wednesday?" was Dietrich's reported reply.

Sharing the screen with Dietrich and Charles Boyer were such character luminaries as Victor (*Mary Hartman, Mary Hartman*) Killian, Lionel (*Hart to Hart*) Stander, and Sam (*Ben Casey*) Jaffe. Unfortunately, the film fell prey to problems at Paramount. Lubitsch was forced to take the fall for the spiraling production costs of *The Big Broadcast* (1938 version) and had been shooting *I Loved a Soldier* with no official budget, no schedule, and no script. Fine movies such as *Casablanca* have been filmed under similar circumstances, and Lubitsch, being a director as well as an executive, was gifted enough to pull it off. Unfortunately, the studio machine—even then—had greater faith in numbers. With Lubitsch gone, the project was shut down, Dietrich unwilling to continue without her current mentor. From January 3 to February 11 of 1936, $900,000 had been spent on what could have been one of the screen's great human transformations.

They don't make 'em like that anymore, and—ultimately—they didn't make this one even then.

The Jimmy Durante Story

Sinatra asked Frank Capra to produce and direct Dean Martin, Bing Crosby, and Sinatra himself in The Jimmy Durante Story.

Celebrity film biographies have always been something of a mixed bag. They were easier to get away with back when the media was not so pervasive, when we didn't have such a good idea of what everyone was like. Once upon a time, you could cast a Doris Day as a Ruth Etting and she didn't have to reach too far outside her Doris Day bag to play it. Even in those days, however, film biographies were often insufficient as both film and biography.

Donald O'Connor is always wonderful, for example, but he is not Buster Keaton. More recently, Robert Downey Jr. managed to look, sound, perhaps even smell like Charlie Chaplin, but he wasn't even remotely funny—one of Chaplin's primary characteristics. And who the hell was Keefe Brasselle, who played the lead in *The Eddie Cantor Story*?

It's impressive to see a star play another star effectively, as when Jimmy Cagney played Lon Chaney in *Man of a Thousand Faces*. But who knows if Cagney got it right?! To all but the most fanatic of citizens, Lon Chaney is just a silent shadow on a silver wall.

James Brolin was not Clark Gable, Rod Steiger was interesting as

W. C. Fields, but even when a star is on the right track it's rare that an "above the title" director becomes attached to a picture of this type.

Does Billy Wilder's *Spirit of St. Louis* count? Charles Lindbergh wasn't exactly the same kind of celebrity that his contemporaries singers Helen Morgan and Lillian Roth (both of whom had pictures made about their lives) were. And Jimmy Stewart was about twenty years too old for the Lindbergh part. It seems that Hollywood and its more distant suburbs have always been getting this kind of thing wrong.

And yet sometimes a combination comes along that is truly sublime, that transcends its elements and has a clear and present magic all its own. A combination such as that which was proposed to film legend Frank Capra back in 1959.

In many respects, 1959 was actually the dawn of the prehippie sixties. Early that year, Frank Sinatra and his Rat Pack were already playing the Sands, filming *Ocean's Eleven,* and fund-raising/carousing with Jack Kennedy. And it was at that time, in the Vegas Sinatra's clan was in the process of inventing, that Sinatra made the offer to Capra.

Capra, the great director of *It Happened One Night, Mr. Smith Goes to Washington,* and *It's a Wonderful Life,* had spent the majority of the fifties making science films for television. Those films, such as *Our Mr Sun* and *Hemo the Magnificent,* were classics of educational entertainment and featured animation, puppets, live action—the works. The critically acclaimed telefilms had been preceded in the forties by Capra's World War II *Why We Fight* films—films that powerfully made the case for the war effort against the nefarious forces of evil. And just as Capra had returned from the war to make *It's a Wonderful Life,* so had he recently retuned from the halls of academia to make *A Hole in the Head.*

A Hole in the Head was a successful fifties comedy starring a rascally Sinatra, Edward G. Robinson as his brother, and young Eddie Hodges as his son. In the film, Sinatra and Hodges introduced the song "High

Hopes," which Sinatra later adapted into the Kennedy campaign theme. So, this fifties Capra/Sinatra collaboration helped usher in the "ring-a-ding-ding" portion of the sixties in which Sinatra was to play such a defining part. And another defining emblem of that era was the team of Frank Sinatra and Dean Martin—singers, pals, co-stars.

In early '59, *Some Came Running,* the first film these cronies made together, had just been released. With the full-fledged Rat Pack classic *Ocean's Eleven* already in production, the tapestry of Kennedy-era pop culture was being cinematically woven when Sinatra called upon Capra to help add another thread to the lounge-culture fabric he was in the process of weaving—a thread from the fabric of an earlier time. Sinatra asked Capra to produce and direct Dean Martin, Bing Crosby, and Sinatra himself in *The Jimmy Durante Story.*

Frank and his co-stars were to play Lou Clayton, Eddie Jackson, and Jimmy Durante, the vaudeville and nightclub performers who defined an earlier era. Capra quoted Sinatra as saying the film would be about "the greatest trio of laugh-getters to ever hit show business."

The project participants had a unique suitability to the task at hand. Capra had been a significant player in the show business of the Durante era, having worked at Mack Sennett's studio and having co-directed the important Harry Langdon feature films. Crosby had been a young pop singer, just coming up at that time. Sinatra had been a kid, influenced by it all, but not to make his mark until the World War II era. And Dino, though just a couple of years younger than Frank, was a postwar icon, just emerging into his definitive era. Together they spanned the show business of the entire century. And the film was to be a celebration of that show business, even as the world was already reeling from Elvis and just a few years away from the arrival of the Beatles, who would change everything forever. *The Jimmy Durante Story* would, in effect, be both a valedictory address and a celebration of a swingin' era that was about to be unswung.

The film, as it developed, was to be a co-production of the stars' production companies, Capra's company, and Columbia Pictures. (Columbia was the studio with which Capra had had the closest relationship during his career—to some degree he made Columbia—so the studio's involvement was yet another nostalgic element of the mix.) Capra called for a meeting of the actors at Puccini's, a Beverly Hills restaurant owned by Sinatra and Peter Lawford, in order to explain the deal. Columbia would put up $5 million, charge no interest, and demand no script approval. Each of the four creative partners would get $250,000 as salary. Durante would get $250 for the rights to his and his partners' life stories (including the book *Schnozzola,* by Gene Fowler). Columbia and the four principal players would each have a one-fifth interest in the film.

The *Hollywood Reporter* of October 2, 1959, announced: "Columbia closes deal for Durante Story 3 star package . . ." And *Variety* claimed the arrangement was "one of the most spectacular deals ever entered into by an independent group."

But there wasn't actually a deal. Negotiations were still going on among the intended participants. In fact, in addition to the lawyers and agents who represented Crosby, Sinatra, Martin, and Capra, there was at one point a fifth law firm added to coordinate things. Meanwhile, Capra moved onto the Columbia lot and started developing the film by himself during a writers' strike. He had to spend his own money when necessary because none of the others would contribute until they had a deal. Capra worked up a 75-page treatment including some dialogue scenes. Finally, on February 15, 1960, a deal was produced for Capra's perusal.

According to this final agreement, any partner could veto any decision, any partner could terminate the deal, every partner had to agree before a bill could be paid—and the three actors didn't even agree to star in the film! They were permitted to offer stars of "equal" magnitude in their stead. Here it was already a year since the project was proposed and this was all it had come to. Capra felt no progress could be made with an arrangement like that and withdrew from the picture.

Louella Parsons reported: "It was Frank Capra's decision to bow out of *The Jimmy Durante Story* . . . " Army Archerd of *Daily Variety* wrote that Capra "couldn't take four producers on one film." Durante said, "We had another problem, too—dose tree guys [Sinatra, Martin, and Crosby] are too busy . . . dey got too many irons in da fire. Da director, Frank Capra, finally quit after waitin' for dem. He couldn't waste his life on da pitcher . . ."

Ironically, it was Durante who had first introduced Sinatra to Capra during the forties. Now, the new ways of doing things, with Sinatra at the vanguard, were preventing these old cronies from celebrating the world they once had known. Independent production, in post–golden age Hollywood, was changing the pace and nature of filmmaking. William Morris Agency head Abe Lastfogel told Capra, "No way you can make a picture today without a star as your partner." But Frank Capra was used to making "Frank Capra films," not complicated deals.

Sinatra, then building his own empire artistically, culturally, and financially, saw things differently. In a letter to his former partners on January 26, 1960, Sinatra wrote: "While Frank Capra was to be the individual producer and director, I always thought of this project as one in which all four of us would make the basic decisions . . ."

Sinatra moved onward and upward into the sixties. After all, there was a Kennedy to elect! Capra, on the other hand, moved upward into his sixties and ultimately retired. Sinatra, interestingly, made a Rat Pack film in 1963 called *Robin and the Seven Hoods*. It was set in the twenties/thirties era and starred Sinatra, Dean Martin, and Bing Crosby. Its intended producer/director, Gene Kelly, left shortly before the start of production. Kelly said, "If you're the producer you're supposed to make the decisions. I was taking orders."

An exasperated Kelly remarked, "Quietly, I like the boys but friendship isn't always everything in this business."

Lover and Friend

She is now more beautiful in every way and more fluent in English and she will enchant more than ever.

After the relative failure of 1941's *Two-Faced Woman,* Greta Garbo decided to leave MGM and her screen career forever.

She just "vanted to be alone."

But that story is just plain untrue. Yes, Garbo left MGM after *Two-Faced Woman.* And yes, she never appeared on the motion picture screen again. But that was not the plan. Garbo had taken time to recalibrate her life. But for a long time that recalibration period was filled with the promise of a renewed career as a movie star.

In fact, by 1948 the prospect of renewal had taken on a certain sense of urgency. Garbo had been trying for a while to put together the elements to make a film based on the life of the French female author who had operated as a man under the name George Sand. The script was to be written by Garbo's friend Salka Viertel. Much activity swirled around the project, and by the summer of '48 independent producer Walter Wanger was making serious inquiries regarding Garbo's readiness to return to the screen. Her answer was that she would be available both "immediately and wholeheartedly."

Garbo, of course, attempted to interest Wanger in the George Sand

project, which had already been
talked up with Selznick, MGM,
Fox, Columbia, J. Arthur Rank,
and Alexander Korda. But Wanger
said that a costume picture would
be too expensive. He suggested a
book titled *The Ballad and the
Source*, which Garbo rejected. She
remained encouraged that the
Sand project could still get off
the ground because Wanger's associate, Eugene Frenke, seemed to
like it.

Meanwhile, agent Leland Hayward seems to have grown weary
of Garbo during her lengthy period
of inactivity. So much so that Salka
Viertel felt Hayward's continued
involvement in Garbo's affairs could actually muck up a pending deal.
George Schlee became Garbo's new representative and structured a
deal with Wanger that stipulated that a film must be made within
one year. The director was to be George Cukor or Carol Reed, and
Garbo was to receive star or first co-star billing.

Since a good many people were rejecting *George Sand,* such esteemed talents as Jean Anouilh, Jean Cocteau, and Sasha Guitry
worked on new ideas for the film. George Cukor opined, "Don't you
think it would be wise if Garbo did not take up her career at the
same point at which she left off—if she struck a new and bold note?"
He suggested *Sappho* as an appropriate project, but Garbo refused,
still wanting to do *George Sand*. Dorothy Parker was hired to work
on the *Sand* script.

On March 15, 1949, however, all concerned decided to abandon
George Sand. They switched to *Honoré de Balzac's La Duchesse de Langeais,* this despite Wanger's previous objection to costume pictures.

Greta Garbo's final film ended in disaster, never to be seen.

The fact that there had been a French-language version of the film in 1947 helped Garbo to see the possibilities in the piece. A treatment was prepared, and Sally Benson, who had written *Meet Me in St. Louis* and Alfred Hitchcock's *Shadow of a Doubt,* was given ten weeks to write the script. There was hope that Edith Piaf might be contracted to sing in the film, and new directorial candidates included Robert Siodmak and Mervyn LeRoy.

The bones of the story are as follows: Antoinette de Navarreins is a denizen of the hedonistic world of the French aristocracy. Having separated from the Duc de Langeais, when she encounters Armand de Montriveau, she is ready for romance. Her manipulations are too much for de Montriveau, and he arranges for a group called the Thirteen to snatch her and reveal her as a temptress. At about this time, however, she realizes she really loves him and her belated realization leads to disaster for all involved.

Famed agent Charles Feldman reportedly told director Irving Rapper, "Garbo will never get off first base with this story," but the project now seemed to be moving ahead smoothly. Garbo shot some test footage with cinematographer Joseph Valentine, but then he died suddenly, and so on May 25, 1949, James Wong Howe and William Daniels did tests with the actress.

Howe said, "You could see this creature just come alive." He utilized just one baby spotlight, and the results are said to have been

spectacular. Bill Daniels photographed her in a more conventional manner, and his report of
the adventure was that "other than
a few laugh wrinkles, her face was
the same." And Garbo is said to
have felt that her eyes were unchanged and that there was a previously unseen depth to her look.

James Wong Howe was hired to
shoot the film, and James Mason
indicated that he would be available as her co-star. Unfortunately,
as the start date approached, it
turned out that screenwriter Benson had been doing a good deal of
drinking and had turned in a very
poor script. A new writer had to be
found and quickly, for the cameras

were to roll in September. Writer/director Max Ophuls was signed
on July 8.

Garbo was told to be in Rome for wardrobe and other production
activities by mid-August. She left, by boat, for Paris on July 15, ar-
riving in Rome to prepare for the shooting of *Lover and Friend* (the
American title) on August 26.

At her hotel she was listed as Miss Harriet Brown, and although
the start date was quickly moved to October, she immediately went
on salary. But now James Mason had become inclined to remain in
LA with his family, and an MGM executive who was involved with
the film likewise stated that he didn't understand why the project
had to be shot in Italy.

The answer, among other things, was that the production needed
Italian money to move forward. And though the cameras weren't

rolling, the producers needed Garbo in Rome to help assure that the money would eventually flow. But now the Italian money was being withheld until the promised American money was put up.

Meanwhile, the only studio space available was being offered by MGM, which was not yet ready to utilize space that they had leased for the production of *Quo Vadis*. But the space had to be used right away, while it was still available, for *Quo Vadis* would eventually need it as well. James Mason, to add to the problems, had finally decided that unless his salary was placed in escrow, he would not do the picture at all.

As Ophuls and Howe arrived in Rome to begin the principal photography, Howard Hughes was being courted to save the film, but he would only put up a portion of the needed funds.

William Morris gave the production a hard deadline for securing James Mason's services.

Sally Benson sued.

The Hollywood Production Code office rejected the script on the grounds that it was immoral.

Garbo was being hounded by the Italian press and had to switch hotels three times. She left for Paris.

As the Italian winter approached, Garbo's mild rheumatism had become a potential problem. The producers understood but held Garbo and her associate Schlee responsible for any resultant financial damages when they agreed to postpone the film until the spring of 1950.

Errol Flynn and Louis Jourdan were now considered to replace James Mason. And Walter Wanger reached a new agreement with Garbo in Paris. She would be paid $16,125 for her time in Rome and also be paid her traveling expenses. By January 1, 1950, Wanger would fully document all financing. And they would publicly make nice with each other.

Wanger announced, "She is now more beautiful in every way and more fluent in English and she will enchant more than ever."

But this was never put to the test because Wanger never documented the production's full financial profile and *Lover and Friend* finally crumbled into ruins.

Here was Greta Garbo, the most luminescent and mysterious of all the stars of the golden era, falling prey to the kind of spit-and-wire film financing constructions that were to become normal in the postwar era. This kind of thing happens all the time today.

And so Garbo inadvertently led the way into the modern world of "independent production," a crazy world responsible for a healthy percentage of the greatest films never made.

"These picture people are a tough lot," said Garbo, "and they lie—they lie all the time. And by their lying, they've wasted a year of my life."

Greta Garbo was to live another forty years of that life, but she never appeared in a motion picture again.

The Lusty Days

One of the great strengths of this extraordinary movie-that-wasn't is that it mixes together elements of the traditional comic Western . . . with a solid storytelling manner reminiscent of Hollywood's golden age.

Samuel Fuller's *The Lusty Days* was a great script in search of life.

Many are the places where one might stumble across a movie that was never made. There are books in which one might chance upon an unexpected nugget. Sometimes you'll find information in a press report. Word of mouth will often do the trick.

And sometimes you find yourself a script.

Movie scripts are available from many sources—the Internet, various Hollywood bookstores, an assortment of mail-order concerns. You might see a stack of 'em on a table somewhere and find your interest piqued by a title you've never heard of—a title that represents a film that was never made. Secretaries, penniless Hollywood hacks, scavengers, and widows are among the character types who funnel screenplays into the marketplace. Because of their ignorance and neediness, script buying can yield some truly great finds.

Last night I found myself reading a script that was handed to me by a friend. The cover read: "The Lusty Days by Samuel Fuller." There was no "Screenplay by" or "Original Screenplay by" or "Written for the Screen by" or even "Written by." It simply said "by Samuel Fuller." This was a good sign. A true professional's lack of pretense is always refreshing in an industry of egos run rampant. And the cover page's simplicity and directness were matched by what I found inside.

The Lusty Days reads like a movie. You see the film while reading the script. There are no extra words, yet all the necessary ones are there. The shots are clear, the characters vivid in the mind's eye. The dialogue is movie-perfect, not an approximation of what some actor will say on the set. You feel as if you can see the look of the film stock as it will be projected on the screen.

The screenplay is filled with the crisp, flowing, impactful entertainment that is the hallmark of the best Hollywood films. You can see the shots clearly even though it is not a shooting script. (A shooting script has all the shots marked numerically.)

The opening sequence is especially terrific. We meet Griff as he pays a small portion of the money he gets from rich boys trying to avoid the Civil War draft to poor men willing to take their place. (It's not as if he wants them to die—he advises them to desert!) When a substitute is killed in the war, his widow's outrage sparks a full-scale riot that takes us through the streets and buildings of New York amid pandemonium and destruction as we meet various characters while the credits roll.

One of the characters we meet is the French entertainer Pompy, a beautiful woman who encounters Griff as the destruction he's caused wreaks havoc upon her environs (and her wardrobe). Griff runs into her again later as he emerges from President Lincoln's office after finagling the lucrative contract to collect the votes from Union soldiers during the upcoming election. Though she attacks Griff upon recognizing him, fate (and Griff's manipulation) throws them together for a good old-fashioned rip-roarin' black comic adventure. They get caught in windstorms, hide in swamps, get arrested behind Confederate lines, put on a "cancan" show in exchange for votes, and even become part of a caravan of escaping slaves on the Underground Railroad—all so that Griff can get back to New York with the votes.

And why does Griff endure all this? For his country? No. He does it for money! The movie is filled with characters of questionable motivation, and it never fully lets them off the hook. The last shot features the "heroic" vote gatherer marching triumphantly into the bank. One of the great strengths of this extraordinary movie-that-wasn't is that it mixes together elements of the traditional comic Western, the darker antihero mode that came into favor during the sixties—even unembarrassed nudity—with a solid storytelling manner reminiscent of Hollywood's golden age.

Sam Fuller's directing credits stretch from *I Shot Jesse James* in 1949, through *Pickup on South Street, Forty Guns, Merrill's Marauders, The Naked Kiss, The Big Red One,* and *White Dog,* all the way to *Day of Reckoning* in 1990. His writing résumé is even more extensive, beginning in 1936 with *Hats Off* and continuing through the years to include 1986's *Let's Get Harry* and 1994's *Girls in Prison.* Fuller has acted in at least twenty-eight films between 1955 and 1997. He even had two cinematography credits. Fuller lived, breathed, and sweated film. He has often been described as a primitive, but though his subject matter was often visceral, it's hard to call a man a primitive who can exert such artistic control over such a complex craft.

After his film *White Dog* (about a dog trained to attack blacks) was misunderstood and essentially shelved back in 1983, Fuller moved to France, where he lived and worked until his return to America during the 1990s. (He received a stellar tribute at Hollywood's American Cinematheque in 1997 and died shortly afterward in October of that year.) It's interesting that the lead characters of *The Lusty Days* are an American man and a Frenchwoman. The Frenchwoman has a more relaxed attitude toward life than the American characters are allowed by their much-vaunted Puritan ethic. But the truly amoral character in the film is the American man. One imagines this reflects Fuller's own life experience.

There's no reason in the world that this movie shouldn't be made even now except for the fact that nobody knows about it or even much cares. Most Hollywood powers are far too busy participating in a bidding war over the latest spec script by a recent film school graduate to concern themselves with an unknown something by a guy who used to be.

Of course, that spec script will be taken out of the hands of its original writer and bear no resemblance to any single being's notions when and if it finally gets made. Meanwhile, *The Lusty Days,* which can be shot as is, would be better than most anything that is released today.

Mein Kampf

Great films, successful films are made in their every detail according to the vision of one man, and through supporting that one man . . .

This passionate assertion of auteurism was made not by a director but by a producer—David. O. Selznick. And he wasn't talking about directors as visionaries and producers as the individuals offering support. The one-man visionary of Selznick's belief was the Producer. (Selznick was, however, willing to allow for the notion of a director/producer.)

Before the sixties or seventies, Selznick's claim would not have been doubted widely. Generally speaking, the director ran things on the set but was not the instigator or overseer of the production.

Directing a studio film was (and is), at base, a job. A director must interpret the script on the set. He must know where to put the camera and how to elicit performances. People often snicker when a different movie wins the Best Picture Oscar from the one that wins Best Director. "How," they ask smugly, "can such and such a film be the best picture and not have the best director?" (Or vice versa.) Well, lots of imperfect pictures show signs of great directorial ability. Likewise, a film may, through some alchemy, be truly great even though it is not, by normal standards, particularly well directed.

By traditional definition, it is the producer's job to develop and oversee a studio picture, down to choosing the director who will interpret the material. A director can be the guiding hand on a project, but then, in effect, he becomes a producer as well. A writer can also guide a project, and then he, in effect, is the producer. Nowadays, we think a director has to be a visionary. (We get bad films from good directors because there's no real producer developing quality material for them to direct.) Generally, great films are one person's vision, and that person can just as reasonably be the producer as the director.

David Selznick is best known as the producer of *Gone with the Wind*, a picture that had many directors, including George Cukor, Victor Fleming (credited), Mervyn LeRoy, and William Cameron Menzies. Yet it has a unity of style reflective of its producer, who guided it over a period of years to its triumphant completion. (Unfortunately, just as directors are now expected to take on responsibilities formerly in the producer's purview, producers are often expected to do *nothing*. The word *producer* is sometimes part of a

One of Hollywood's greatest producers of all time, David O. Selznick— ironically a Jew—sought to bring Hitler's life story *Mein Kampf* to the screen during World War II.

vanity credit, bestowed via negotiations on various unworthies and flunkies. We now use the term *line producer* to describe a per-

The rights to Hitler's *Mein Kampf* were reserved by David O. Selznick in an effort to bring the dictator's story to the screen.

son who does many of the tasks once handled by a simple "producer.")

Most producers have never been true visionaries; neither have most directors and writers. But just as some directors are transcendent artists, some producers are the truly great authors of their films. Aside from Walt Disney, the producer most frequently regarded as the unequivocal auteur is David O. Selznick. Like Disney, Selznick was a producer beyond the normal meaning of the term. Though he began his career in the 1920s, Selznick was a second-generation Hollywood power. (His father had been a producer.) Abandoning studio work, Selznick became a pioneering independent producer. He also pioneered movie packaging, co-productions, international co-productions, and wide movie openings. In the movie world, he was a business visionary as well as a creative visionary.

On his personal productions, the director was not allowed to film a sequence before Selznick was called to the set to approve the camera position. (In this sense, Selznick was really a supervising director as well as producer.) He micromanaged and was known for lengthy memos, many of which were collected posthumously in a successful book edited by Rudy Behlmer.

In addition to *Gone with the Wind*, Selznick produced such films as *Dinner at Eight, Anna Karenina,* the original *A Star Is Born, The*

Prisoner of Zenda, Nothing Sacred, Intermezzo, Spellbound, and *Duel in the Sun.* He was instrumental in the production of *The Third Man* and *A Farewell to Arms.* Despite his penchant for control, he nurtured producer/directors like Alfred Hitchcock and let them do their own thing.

Selznick's mania for detail got him into difficulties. When World War II broke out, many of his peers were pressed into important wartime service. Darryl F. Zanuck (a fellow middle-initial guy) became a colonel in charge of film productions for the army, and Jack L. Warner was a lieutenant colonel in the air force. When Undersecretary of the Navy James V. Forrestal presented Selznick to Secretary of the Navy Frank Knox regarding a similar job, he felt the need to refer to the producer as an "egomaniac." Unable to leave it alone, Selznick wrote Forrestal a letter addressing the issue and, not surprisingly, did not get the job.

Selznick, however, felt passionate about assisting the war effort, and the producer knew his best opportunities were through his knowledge of film. As a result, an amazing movie, the likes of which we have never seen, became Selznick's highest priority just four days after America entered the war!

On December 11, 1941, Selznick wired his story editor, Katherine Brown:

To Miss Katherine Brown

Immediately upon your receipt of this wire please drop everything and rush over to the Hays office to register "Mein Kampf" as well as anything else necessary to protect it, such as "Life of Adolph Hitler" and "My Life, by Adolph Hitler." I hope there will be no nonsense about whether this is copyrighted or noncopyrighted work, and I hope the Hays office has the good sense to realize that I consider it noncopyrighted and have no intention of buying rights or paying royalties, which in circumstances would of course be ridiculous. Even before we were at war, publishers considered it in these

*terms. . . . keep it utterly secret until I have had the opportunity to
check with Washington on the making of this film. . . . will await
wired word from you but better address me to my home to further
guard secrecy, and please caution not to leave any wires concerning
it around the desks, and not to even discuss it with people in our
own organization. . . . for purposes of wires and letters suggest you
refer to it as "Tales from History."*

Selznick was considering the great Ben Hecht as the screenwriter
and Alfred Hitchcock as the director. The war era brought us cartoons
and comedies featuring a silly-looking Hitler and ratlike Japanese,
but a serious wartime treatment of the enemy leadership was rarely,
if ever, committed to film. Making these figures seem smaller through
ridicule was the choice that America's ministers of propaganda either
were saddled with or embraced. But wouldn't it have been amazing
to have confronted the serious depth of our enemy's evil in a first-
class production by David O. Selznick? How harrowing would a film
about Hitler by Hitchcock have been?

Mein Kampf ("My Struggle"), written by a younger Hitler while he
was in prison, presented his life story (as he wanted it told), his
philosophies, his plans for the future. It was instrumental in his rise.
Selznick could have splashed across the screen the twisted, evil soul
of America's nemesis, not in the manner of an exploitation producer
but in the manner of a serious film artist with an understanding of
the mainstream audience. Look at how true cinematic art was used
to further Hitler's own goals via *Triumph of the Will* and *Olympia*.
Great serious filmmaking could have served America's goals as well.

But that was not the way we chose to go. It's too bad Selznick had
to check with Washington before proceeding with his efforts. (Even
his reputation as an egomaniac would have stood him in good stead
when transferring the life of a megalomaniac to the screen.) But
though we were deprived of an artful work of American cinematic
propaganda, we did, of course, win the war. And maybe enemies, we

could laugh at helped embolden us to defeat them. Burlesque Nazis may not populate the finest cinematic art, but they made America laugh during a difficult time.

Sorry, Mr. Selznick. But thank you, Moe.

The Merry Widow

Imagine, if you will, the quality of The Magic Flute *combined with the crossover appeal and talent of Barbra Streisand at her peak in the 1970s.*

Ingmar Bergman has directed some of the world's most compelling human dramas—*Wild Strawberries, Persona, Fanny and Alexander, Scenes from a Marriage* . . . While I daresay few Americans could name another Swedish film director, the one we can name is one of the greatest directors in the world.

This writer/director/producer is perceived by many as a maker of dense, somber fare—the kind of film you pretend to like when trying to impress a particularly sophisticated date. In truth, since the 1940s Bergman has directed a wide variety of projects for film, television, and theater. Justifiably regarded as a true artist of the cinema, he has created an oeuvre that encompasses everything from opera, to dark comedy, to the most intense film drama, to life-affirming love fests.

Like most filmmakers, Bergman has developed projects that have never been made. One involved the great Italian director Federico Fellini. Bergman has been reported as saying that Fellini's work had a "seductive quality of mesmerizing your attention" and that "even if you're not in full agreement with what he says, you enjoy the way he says it." When Bergman and then-companion Liv Ullmann spent six weeks in Rome in 1968, Bergman met Fellini for the first time. Ull-mann reported that Fellini and Bergman "embraced, laughed together as if they had lived the same life. They wandered through the streets in the night, arms around each other, Fellini wearing a dramatic black cape, Ingmar in his little cap and an old winter coat." Fellini, according to Bergman, had a "way of seeing the world with such intensity." Bergman considers Fellini "one of the most complete cinematographic creators I have ever seen."

It should, therefore, come as no surprise that upon meeting, the two quickly decided they wanted to work together. They planned to collaborate on a film titled *Love Duet,* which was tentatively scheduled to begin filming in Stockholm and Rome in the autumn of 1969. Fellini asserted that there would be no game playing between the two auteurs, reportedly saying the production would "not be a poker game in which we hide aces up our sleeves." (He joked that the only person the two would hide things from would be the producer.)

Costumes were conceptualized. Actresses Katharine Ross and Viveca Lindfors were queried as to their availability. By 1970, however, with the project still in development, Bergman (who had become immersed in other endeavors) unilaterally canceled the project.

But only a couple of years later, Bergman embarked upon another (and perhaps his most interesting) "might-have-been." While making his first English-language film, *The Touch* (1971), Bergman became acquainted through star Elliott Gould with one Barbra Streisand. (Gould is Streisand's ex-hubby.) Streisand's talent and bankability were not lost on the director, and the two began discussing the idea of doing a project together. On December 1, 1972, a press conference was held at Svenske Filmindustri to announce that Streisand would star in Bergman's adaptation of Franz Lehar's 1905 operetta, *The Merry Widow.*

The plot involved a certain Count Danilo and his romancing of a "merry" widow. But the primary appeal of operettas, and the musical comedies into which they evolved, has always been music and spectacle. Because of said music and/or spectacle, *The Merry Widow* has been adapted by some of the best directors in movie history (though they played fast and loose with the story points).

The first Hollywood version was directed by Erich von Stroheim during the silent era. (The film did include *"The Merry Widow Waltz."*) It was remade more than once—notably by Ernst Lubitsch in 1934 (starring Jeanette MacDonald and Maurice Chevalier).

Bergman himself had enjoyed a major success with the piece as a young stage director. His production featured cancan dancers on a horseshoe-shaped bridge and French perfume sprayed into the auditorium. A witness reported that the production was determinedly nonironic, that Bergman treated the "fairy-tale world, on the contrary, with a kind of tender respect." *The Merry Widow* was the most popular show in the ten years the enormous Malmö Municipal Theater had been in business.

Bergman planned a lavish cinematic treatment as well, with 100 dancers utilized in important sequences. Unfortunately, Bergman ended up unable to afford even 35. The '73 oil crisis wreaked havoc upon available funds. Dino De Laurentiis offered $4 million but would not agree to cover cost overruns. Bergman had a policy of refusing to compromise once a budget had been established, and one day he reportedly said, ". . . let's drop this project." He had worked on it for eight months (not including the screenplay he had written as early as 1954).

It's hard to say which of the principals would have benefited more from the completion of this project. Though Streisand is clearly cinematically ambitious, it would have been truly satisfying to see her in an "artistic" project at a time when her persona (no pun intended) was more accessible. Bergman, on the other hand, soon directed 1975's *The Magic Flute*. He felt that *The Merry Widow* and *The Magic Flute* were "two branches on the same tree, and they are both very green, and the flowers are very beautiful."

The Magic Flute is considered by some to be one of Bergman's greatest works. At this point in his career, he was strongly oriented toward committing this kind of material to film. Imagine, if you will, the quality of *The Magic Flute* combined with the crossover appeal and talent of Barbra Streisand at her peak in the 1970s. This was the potential of the Bergman/Streisand *The Merry Widow.*

"You have to be careful with Lehar music," Bergman once asserted. "It's pure gold."

When the money became scarce, Bergman—appropriately careful—avoided recklessness. He protected Lehar and the audience from experiencing anything less than perfection.

Bergman's quest for perfection tells us what might have been.

Napoleon

He fascinates me. His life has been described as an epic poem of action.

That great directors are a lot like great generals is self-evident. Therefore, it stands to reason that some of the great directors might express an interest in and admiration for some of the great military men. On September 23, 1968, the French newspaper *L'Express* reported that "several hundred books on Napoleon [had been] . . . shipped to the London office of Stanley Kubrick." *2001: A Space Odyssey* was finally in release, and Kubrick told his associate, Bob Gaffney, "I'm going to start a project and my next project is on the life of Napoleon."

Kubrick later reported: "He fascinates me. His life has been described as an epic poem of action." Kubrick believed Napoleon "was one of those rare men who move history and mold the destiny of their own times and generations to come. In a very concrete sense, our own world is the result of Napoleon, just as the physical and geographic map of Europe is the result of World War II." Most important, Kubrick believed that "there has never been a good or accurate movie about him." He felt that Abel Gance's *Napoleon,* for example, was technically impressive, but its content did not appeal to him.

"This will not be just a dusty historic pageant," Kubrick announced. He went on to say that "the sheer drama and force of Napoleon's life is a fantastic subject for a film biography." And Kubrick felt the relationship between Napoleon and Josephine was "one of the great obsessional passions of all time."

Kubrick's research encompassed accounts from Napoleon's own time. He broke down all his research material into categories and could even tell you the weather on the day of a specific battle. He hired as consultant a professor from Oxford University who had been studying Napoleon for thirty-five years.

Location scouts looked into the suitability and availability of sites in France, Italy, Romania, Czechoslovakia, and Hungary. At home in England, Kubrick blew up to wall-size a nineteenth-century painting of a Napoleon battle and placed over it a grid composed of one-inch squares. He counted the number of painted soldiers in each square in order to figure out the number of soldiers in Napoleon's army.

The Romanian government was told that the production wanted seventy-five thousand troops in the field. Kubrick and his camera crew were intending to fly over an army of fifteen to thirty thousand troops and some five thousand horses. They were looking to shoot in a country that would lease them its army. Kubrick's team had to find locations that were near existing army bases so that the soldiers would have someplace to stay and could be transported efficiently to the set. One country under consideration supposedly talked about drafting soldiers to meet the filmmaker's needs. The director planned to fly in forty thousand gallons of flu vaccine to protect against sickness-induced shut-down. And he ordered twenty thousand gallons of fake blood.

Kubrick planned to stage the battles in "a vast tableau where the formations moved in almost choreographic fashion. It's necessary," he said, "to re-create all the conditions of battle with painstaking accuracy.

"Napoleonic battles are so beautiful," Kubrick explained, "that it's worth every effort to explain the configuration to an audience . . . [The battles] all have an aesthetic brilliance that doesn't require a military mind to appreciate. . . . It's almost like a great piece of music or the purity of a mathematical formula. It's the quality I want to bring across, as well as the sordid reality of battle."

Kubrick thought that it would probably be a long film, as it was to cover Napoleon's entire life. "I haven't set any specific guidelines on length," he asserted. "I believe that if you have a truly interesting film, it doesn't matter how long it is."

Exterior location work was scheduled for the winter of 1969. It was expected to take two to three months to complete, followed by three to four months of studio work. The production team needed four thousand costumes and considered using a special, extra-strong Du Pont fabric on which you could actually print period designs for about two-fifty a pop.

Meanwhile, another Napoleon movie, *Waterloo*, starring Rod Steiger, was shooting at about the same time. Competition between the two units was keen, and some Europeans who were considering abetting the Kubrick flick were reportedly told, "If you work with these people [the Kubrick team], we're going to kill you." It was as if some of the aggressive and competitive spirit of the characters they were chronicling had rubbed off on the filmmakers themselves.

Still, it wasn't the competition with another film that killed the project—it was the massive expense that the undertaking would require. United Artists, for instance, was interested in the film, but the cost was just too much for them. Kubrick figured an American studio would have to borrow money at almost 20 percent interest to cover the budgetary requirements of the film. Apparently feeling he had no other reasonable choice, Kubrick canceled the effort.

And when Kubrick canceled the project, audiences not only lost out on the opportunity to see the spectacle I've just described; they also lost the opportunity to see a potentially fascinating evocation of the Napoleon character. Because the man Kubrick wanted to play the Gallic emperor was none other than his future *Shining* star, Jack Nicholson. "[Kubrick's] gotten me into the character," said Nicholson. "I've done research and all that kind of stuff."

But that research was not to be utilized, at least not on this project. Kubrick went on to make *A Clockwork Orange* as his next picture,

Stanley Kubrick had his eye on the story of Napoleon for quite some time and planned the epic to be his follow-up to *2001: A Space Odyssey.* Kubrick planned to hire 75,000 Romanian soldiers to depict Napoleon's army in sweeping battle scenes.

and we are left once again to wonder what might have been. There have, of course, been other abandoned Kubrick projects. *AI* (which stands for "artificial intelligence") was pushed aside in favor of *Eyes Wide Shut* at least in part because of the huge technological challenge it would have entailed. Kubrick's untimely death has left a void in the industry and a great epic unproduced.

National Lampoon's Jaws 3, People 0

In the picture's opening sequence, Jaws *author Peter Benchley is eaten by a shark in his swimming pool before finishing the script for* Jaws 3.

Universal Pictures was a pioneer in combining series franchises to enhance creativity and extend commercial life. When it was no longer viable to present Frankenstein *or* the Wolfman, Frankenstein *met* the Wolfman. In the film industry it's called new wine, old bottle—in this case, it's clue mixing drinks, which often leads to unpredictable results.

By the late seventies, Universal had rocked the industry with its *Jaws* movies (continuing the studio's experiments in horror) and *National Lampoon's Animal House* (an Abbott and Costella type picture for the modern era). When *Jaws 2* demonstrated that there might not be much life left in the shark-laden well, the studio decided to combine its popular franchises of the seventies. The good people at *National Lampoon* were given the opportunity to make the third *Jaws* movie, and the planned result was *National Lampoon's Jaws 3, People 0.*

The script, with story by *Lampoon* publisher Matty Simmons himself, is clearly the work of people in love with what they're doing. It's possessed of youth and newness and talent and ambition and a real understanding of comedy and a desire to make people laugh—to make themselves laugh.

The screenwriters are (in reverse order) Tod Carroll and John Hughes. Just as *Lampoon* veteran Doug Kenney embraced the cinema when he wrote *Animal House,* so did Hughes and Carroll when given the opportunity to make *Jaws 3, People 0.* Hughes was to make his mark later with *National Lampoon's Vacation* and, of course, his definitive youth comedies of the eighties.

The thing is, *J3P0* is barely a *Jaws* picture at all. *Jaws 3, People 0* is a wild comedy about a movie studio trying to make *Jaws 3* amid vicious jockeying for power. The screenplay uses its scenario as an excuse to careen into virtually all the comic territory its authors can discover.

In the picture's opening sequence, *Jaws* author Peter Benchley is eaten by a shark in his swimming pool before finishing the script for *Jaws 3.* Soon thereafter, the aging head of Mecca Studios is also killed by a shark, as if the killer fish have decided they don't want another *Jaws* picture to be released. The mogul's will says the studio now belongs to a woman he met once on location in Idaho. She arrives in Hollywood just in time to get involved in a vicious fight for control of Mecca.

Her boy Sonny is entrusted with the direction of *Jaws 3,* starring fat leading man Butch Peluso. The co-writer of the film is a bell captain Sonny met at a hotel, and in light of *Star Wars'* success, the two decide *Jaws 3*'s sharks should be visitors from space. A Jacques Cousteau type is on call to make certain the entire project is not ended by sharks while enemy studio henchman try to ensure that it is.

The characters have silly names and do silly things There is a neat little story, and on it are hung comic pleasures that made me laugh out loud.

Here is the Cousteau character's description of the cause of the studio head's death:

COCKATOO
Mr. Canterberry was thoroughly eaten by a legitimate, 100% shark in the category of the great number-2 gray marine shark which is simultaneously identical to the same shark who had a mouthful of your Mr. Benchley in addition also.

Later he offers a cigarette from his cigarette case to a visitor from the studio:

COCKATOO
Have I presented yourself with a cigarette from my pocket tobacco cabinet, today?

Yeah, I know—inept English from silly foreigners, yadda, yadda, yadda . . . *but it's funny!* The whole damn script is filled with rhythm and whimsy and is just plain *funny. Jaws 3, People 0,* written by the generation that grew up in an America without the politically correct gene, is a perfect mixture of nuts-and-bolts construction and seventies abandon. It has cameo appearances by such as (then) surviving vaudevillian George Jessel plus drugs and breasts a-poppin'—a wondrous combination, reflective of its moment in time.

Plus, it's a fairly savage indictment of Hollywood.

In the wake of their *Animal House* success, the Lampooners were obviously having a lot of interaction with Hollywood types as they pondered their next project. Still outsiders, the Lampooniacs were seemingly mortified by what they found.

Jaws 3, People 0 shows us a Hollywood of horrifyingly vicious executives, morally bankrupt old men, and hot babe/whores who'll do anything for a career. Still, the folks at *Lampoon,* being new to this, were in many ways represented in *J3P0* by the characters who came to Hollywood from Idaho. They learned much of what they knew about Hollywood from the movies themselves. So we end up with a movie that is part personal observation, part Jerry Lewis's *The*

Errand Boy. The result was yet another opportunity to segue from old to new, to bring film comedy as we once knew it into the new era.

Instead, we ended up with the lackluster *Jaws 3-D* (part of a minitrend, along with *Friday the 13th 3-D*). It was a reasonable choice for Universal to make, because you only get one chance to do the double-meaning 3-D title thing. On the other hand, you can always make *Jaws 4, People 0.*

But they didn't. For John Hughes, by the time of his eighties success this opportunity was gone. He did some important stuff, to be sure. He helped define a generation with *The Breakfast Club.* Increasingly, however, he became more like the guys he and Carroll so savagely lampoon in this script.

John Hughes is a mogul now.

Lampoon made more movies, Hughes made movies, Universal made movies, and things went on more or less as before. But when a funny script like this is left on the shelf, it's the audience that suffers, because we need all the laughs we can get. I don't know what the score is on the studio side, but in cases like this, the audience ends up with nothing.

Nostromo

Silberman wanted Lean to sign a document saying that if he died or became incapacitated, they could still call Nostromo *"A David Lean Film."*

When David Lean, the director of epics like *The Bridge on the River Kwai* and *Lawrence of Arabia*, appeared before the Cambridge Film Society in 1985, its members voted for *Nostromo* as the story they most wanted him to tackle next. (The Joseph Conrad novel had also been recommended to him years earlier by his longtime screenwriter, Robert Bolt.) Lean had not completed a film in the almost fifteen years between the 1970 release of *Ryan's Daughter* and the then-recent release of *A Passage to India.* Though now well into his seventies, he didn't waste another minute before beginning the process that he hoped would lead to another film. He decided to read *Nostromo.*

The book took a long time to engage him, but when it did it engaged him thoroughly. He wrote: "If only I could free myself from present-day screen conventions, I could put this into a flow of pictures." He decided to call Steven Spielberg, who immediately agreed to produce the film for Warner Bros. Lean was estranged from Robert Bolt, so he engaged Christopher Hampton to collaborate on the screenplay.

The book revolved around a silver mine and the silver's effect on the characters. As Lean told one inquirer, "The villain is money." The opening image of the film was quickly conceived—one of the characters was to be sitting at the bottom of the sea with silver coming out of his pockets.

Hampton said of Lean, "He was very stimulating to work with because so much energy went into the work. He would attack a scene quite ferociously in terms of insisting that it didn't simply carry information, that it somehow moved the story forward." Hampton believed this came from Lean's early experience as a film editor.

Alan Rickman was tested for the film. Paul Scofield and Isabella Rossellini were offered roles. European actor George Correface was tested at Shepperton Studios with costumes, sets, and even other actors! (Perfectionist Lean had the test done over because he didn't like the lighting.)

David Lean would spend years trying to bring *Nostromo* to the screen, only to be struck down by ill health.

Lean went to Mexico to photograph locations for the film. He was willing to forgo his salary if necessary to get the film made in 70mm. (No movie was shot in 70mm between Lean's own *Ryan's Daughter* and Ron Howard's 1992 *Far and Away*.) In general, Lean wanted to style the cinematography after Preston Sturges's *Sullivan's Travels* (1941).

Lean intended to light a scene that took place in darkness as if with only ambient phosphorescence, the light of the stars, and the silver themselves. During a lovemaking scene, the light from a lighthouse was to come around every few seconds to reveal the characters in a different stage of the game. And there would also be flashback sequences tinted blue as in silent days.

A memo from Spielberg dated February 13, 1987, read: "*Nostromo* is written so well, it is somewhat embarrassing for me to make any suggestions about how to improve it." Still, he did raise a few points. However, he signed off by saying: "I hope these notes do not frustrate you beyond Excedrin."

But the memo left Lean enraged. Spielberg had indicated to Lean that he was his hero. Lean didn't want notes; he wanted Spielberg to facilitate the production of the film and get out of the way. Eventually, Spielberg did get out of the way . . . by abandoning the project completely. Lean said, "I shall probably be eighty before we start making this film."

Meanwhile, Christopher Hampton had facilitated a reunion between Lean and Bolt. When the two finally talked, "a look of joy radiated from Robert," said Hampton. Bolt amicably replaced Hampton as Lean's collaborator.

Bolt, the great writer of such films as *Lawrence of Arabia,* had suffered a stroke and had problems with his speech, but Lean happily and accurately interpreted his intentions. Lean said of Bolt, "He started to spark right away." Bolt decided to make the film less about money and more about *Nostromo.*

But just when things seemed to be percolating along, Lean was struck by the first of what became a chain of infirmities. In January of '89, Lean came down with shingles. The steroids he was prescribed caused myopathy. Lean had trouble moving. He also had abnormal liver function.

Oddly, the prescription for this was more steroids . . . and they worked! By Christmas 1989, Lean was significantly better.

Still, he wrote to Bolt: "I have been thinking quite a lot about death. The other evening, a great flight of geese passed by my window in the half dark. I did not even see them. It was the swoosh of their wings, beautiful but doom-laden, which arrested me."

But even in deep communion with his mortality, the director funneled his feelings into his work. He wrote: "At the end of the film, I
would like to try bringing in the sound of the goose wings just before
Nostromo dies in the Paio. Even show Mrs. Gould and Nostromo
looking upward listening to their passing."

With Spielberg gone, Lean formed a partnership with Serge Silberman, who had produced Buñuel films. Silberman wanted Lean to
sign a document saying that if he died or became incapacitated, they
could still call Nostromo "A David Lean Film." Lean refused, and apparently Silberman got nasty. Lean realized that Silberman, with
about $2 million of his own money in the film, had a lot at stake.
But the encounter left Lean "absolutely shattered."

Lean went to LA to receive the AFI Lifetime Achievement Award,
and though he had been using a wheelchair, he managed to summon
up the strength to make a grand entrance and walk about forty feet
to his table. His speech contained a rebuke of the artist-squelching
tendencies of the money people, and at least one studio executive
was personally offended. Hallelujah.

Lean returned to work on the film and found that his insurance
premium was higher than his fee. The money people insisted on a
standby director in case Lean became unable to finish the film. Those
in contention included John Boorman, Peter Yates, Arthur Penn, and
Kevin Costner. Lean preferred Robert Altman. They chose James
Bond director Guy Hamilton.

A friend asked Lean, "Why on earth do you have to do this film?
You're wealthy enough. You don't need to do it." Lean replied, "I
have to. It's in my blood."

Lean now decided he didn't like many of Robert Bolt's ideas and
took over the scriptwriting chores himself. Then he was diagnosed
with cancer. A friend described his attitude as, "We'll forget the film
and go enjoy life and wait till I die," followed by, "I don't want to
die. Maybe I can still do the film if I get better."

Lean underwent radiation treatments for his cancer. Eventually,
he was told that the sets for Nostromo were being torn down. He died

on April 16, 1991. At the funeral, Serge Silberman said, "The sets were all built; everything was ready!"

But David Lean had lost his tenacious battle to make one last film—a gigantic epic film like the ones that came before it. By this point, a David Lean film was by definition a great film. Some people thought he was the greatest filmmaker ever. Even the fifteen years between *Ryan's Daughter* and *A Passage to India* failed to rob him of his gift. But he could not escape his own mortality, the inevitable conclusion of his own epic life.

The Ripping Friends

They think superheroes are wimps because they have to cheat to win their battles—how manly are you if you have a superpower? You could beat the crap out of anyone! That's not very manly. A manly guy will take the pain along with the victory. It's got to hurt to win—that's The Ripping Friends.

One of the greatest scripts I ever encountered was one that I never actually read. *The Ripping Friends* was performed for me as a one-man show complete with all the acting, music, voices, and sound effects, including farts. All these sounds and gases burst out of one of the few people I can truly feel confident calling a creative genius— John Kricfalusi (last name pronounced cris-fa-loos-ee, just like it's spelled). John K. (as he is commonly known) is the creator of *Ren & Stimpy* and is one of the people responsible for the resurgence of animation both theatrically and on television. I had the rare treat of watching him "pitch the board." Basically, this is when an animator becomes a storyteller, walking an audience (usually a bunch of development executives) through the film while showing storyboards and doing all the voices and sound. But when John K. pitches, he becomes so passionately involved that he sweats profusely and his glasses come flying off as he spits all over. It's exhausting just to watch him do it.

Few would deny that John Kricfalusi's manic sensibilities are destined for the big screen. And if John K. has his way, his project *The Ripping Friends* will take him there. "It's about the world's most manly men, who win their battles through sheer, raw manliness and willpower," says the animator of his story's title characters. "They don't have superpowers, but they have the suits. They think superheroes are wimps because they have to cheat to win their battles—how manly are you if you have a superpower? You could beat the crap out of anyone! That's not very manly. A manly guy will take the pain along with the victory. It's got to hurt to win—that's *The Ripping Friends*."

Kricfalusi tries his best to explain the nuances of character construction to someone who has trouble rendering stick figures: "Ren and Stimpy are different character structures than what people are used to; they're not based on the Disney clichéd construction. Most animators cannot draw human anatomy; they draw Disney anatomy, which is an abstraction—it's not based on anything real. The Ripping Friends have this caricatured human anatomy, which is very hard to draw."

Kricfalusi clearly has an affinity for his superhero characters, each modeled after gruff thespians like Marlon Brando, Peter Graves, and Kirk Douglas. "They work out on their pain machines every morning," he continues. "They strap themselves to it and all it does is give them horrible pain for an hour—screaming at the top of their lungs. They love it!"

The story involves a group of superheroes who are also scientists. They have an assistant, Jimmy the hapless boy, a Forrest Gump–type character: "The Ripping Friends live in a superindustrialized complex that they built with their own sweat and blood called R.I.P.C.O.T., which stands for the Really Impressive Prototype City Of next Tuesday. The only thing that ever defeated the Ripping Friends is the laws of nature. They can't break through time, and they are trying to find a way to get through it."

The Ripping Friends are so distraught at their failure to conquer time that they begin to punch directly at the space in front of them and suddenly find a way to *rip* through time. They rip through the very fabric of time itself and are taken on a trip through Earth's past. When they find themselves in a prehistoric landscape complete with early sea creatures we observe the first animal to take steps on land—evolution taking place before our very eyes. Then it is accidentally killed by our heroes. Evolution has been literally stopped in its tracks, and the heroes must use their unique abilities to save the day. The fate of the future of the Earth is at stake!

While pitching his story around Hollywood, Kricfalusi has been surprised by Hollywood's lack of imagination: "Every movie studio calls me and says, 'You should be making movies,' but I know it's a lie. Because I know when I bring 'em something new they're going to say, 'Well, wait a minute; this isn't *Ren and Stimpy*.' No, this is a new idea! You would swear all these guys had never seen a movie earlier than 1985."

Even Disney called John K. for a pitch session. They loved his ideas, but a deal was never struck. "It's a really ambitious project," he says, "and I'm afraid of that because I know I'm going to be battling with studio executives. The other battle is . . . it's too fuckin' hard to draw!"

Having budgeted the project at about $25 million, Kricfalusi intends to use the latest animation technology in *The Ripping Friends*. In fact, while the two-dimensional artwork of the characters is stunning in its manliness, Kricfalusi's more recent thinking is to do the entire film in three-dimensional computer animation like *Toy Story*.

But while animation technology has evolved, cartoonists haven't. "Animators are inbred," Kricfalusi says. "They're only influenced by Disney, who grew up in this vacuum. How do I get animators who can draw well enough that they can draw more than one character, let alone characters that act differently? The Disney movies have maybe ten expressions that every character does: anger, happiness, sadness. There's no subtle, complex emotions."

In order to bring his unique vision to the screen, Kricfalusi will probably endure a fair amount of pain himself.

The Road to Tomorrow

Crosby's forehead was gushing blood, but he hadn't lost his sense of humor. He said, "I'll have to get a new finish to my act!"

Bob Hope and Bing Crosby's *Road* pictures are remembered as breezy, irreverent, and even hip. Though first titled *The Road to Mandalay* and slated to star Fred MacMurray and Jack Oakie, 1940's *The Road to Singapore* established a comic relationship among the male stars and Dorothy Lamour that would sustain a series of seven pictures, all the way to the Kenne-

dy era. Of course, the films had gotten a little stale by the time they made *The Road to Hong Kong* in '62. The Hollywood that bred the series had largely disappeared since the production of the previous entry, *The Road to Bali,* and *Hong Kong* was the only *Road* picture not made by Paramount Pictures. It was, as was becoming increasingly popular, produced independently and released by United Artists. Also, Bing Crosby had aged visibly since the previous entry and, on top of that, didn't think Dorothy Lamour was young enough to play the love interest anymore. (A young Joan Collins ended up in the traditional Lamour role, though Bob made sure Lamour was in the picture.)

By the end of the 1960s, age was wreaking havoc with Hope's solo films as well. It wasn't just that he was becoming out of step with the times; it was the star vanity at play. Hope's daughter Linda, who has produced many of his projects, has said that she long wanted her dad to do a film that showed him as he really was—as an aging man unlikely to win the leggy and busty pinup types he continued to favor as sketch partners. Elliot Kozak, who produced Hope's pictures for years, has stated that Hope routinely turned down such scripts. He either hasn't seen himself or hasn't wanted the world to see him in that way. There's a scene in Hope's last theatrical film to date, 1972's *Cancel My Reservation,* wherein Keenan Wynn's character asks Hope how old he is. The nearly seventy-year-old Hope replies, without a hint of irony, "Forty-two." Suspension of disbelief is one thing, but this is ridiculous!

That's why the idea that was generated after Hope, Crosby, and Lamour reunited for the first time since '62 at the 1976 Thalians Ball was so exciting. The threesome decided to do a *Road* picture that would feature them as grandparents, reflecting them the way they were in their advancing years and with the potential to extract comedy as genuine as in youthful days of yore. The film was the brainchild of Ben Starr, who had co-written 1969's Bob Hope/Jackie Gleason starrer, *How to Commit Marriage,* which was a fairly sophisticated film for its time about sixties social and sexual mores that made money at the height of the hippie era. There was, therefore, reason to believe Starr was capable of the blend of contemporary and classic required for this film. An enthusiastic Hope and Crosby quickly optioned the property from Starr, whereupon Hope talked British entertainment tycoon Sir Lew Grade into producing it.

The film was scheduled to begin principal photography in the fall of 1977, after Crosby's summer tour. Its slight plot, in the tradition of the series, hinged upon the trio's inadvertent involvement in an international mystery. Hope was to run into Crosby at the airport as, coincidentally, both were taking their grandchildren to London. This was the era of such family fare as *The Muppet Movie* (in which Hope has a cameo), and the family angle would likely have held great commercial appeal.

Hope was experiencing a resurgence and would shortly be honored by the Film Society of Lincoln Center and treated to a documentary tribute made by Woody Allen, titled *My Favorite Comedian*. Bing Crosby was experiencing a career resurgence as well. He was no longer just the guy who did Christmas specials and orange juice commercials, as his stock with the young was growing. The year 1977 was when he performed his famous duet with David Bowie. A

The Road to Tomorrow would have reunited Hope and Crosby in their final and biggest road film ever.

college radio programmer in Albany, New York, was that year enthused by only two song stylists—Elvis Costello and Bing Crosby! Crosby had resumed an active concert schedule, and his reviews were positively glowing. In short, this was the moment to make this film.

On March 3, 1997, Crosby taped an all-star salute to his fifty years in show business at the Ambassador Auditorium in Pasadena, California. At the conclusion of the show, as he was taking his bows, he fell twenty feet into the orchestra pit. Hope was the first to reach Crosby's side. Crosby's forehead was gushing blood, but he hadn't lost his sense of humor. He said, "I'll have to get a new finish to my act!" Just as fellow Hollywoodite Ronald Reagan told jokes after being shot, Crosby sang in the ambulance on the way to the hospital.

His recovery was slow and *The Road to Tomorrow* (which at some point became *The Road to the Fountain of Youth*) was delayed. He did ultimately recover, however, and he made that European tour. After finishing an engagement in England during which he uncharacteristically told the audience, "I love you," Crosby flew to Spain for some relaxation. On the eighteenth hole of a Spanish golf course, Bing Crosby died of a heart attack on October 18, 1977.

At the time of Crosby's death, Hope had ironically been preparing a television special titled *The Road to Hollywood.* It was replaced by a tribute to his longtime partner and friend. Some months later, Hope was hosting the 50th Annual Academy Awards when winner Bert Schneider chose to make some disparaging comments about America's involvement in Vietnam. The old militant fire kicked in, and Hope told the worldwide audience that the Academy didn't agree with what Schneider had said.

The next day, screenwriter Ben Starr called Hope to talk about ideas for the *Road* picture, which after Crosby's death was to co-star George Burns instead. Hope bragged about his stance on the awards, and Starr told him that he was wrong, that not all Academy members agreed with his position. For a while thereafter, Hope was not available to take Starr's calls. But one day Starr phoned and Hope said, "How long will it take you to get to the house?"

But the moment had already passed. Dorothy Lamour is now dead. George Burns is gone, too. Bob hasn't made any additional theatrical pictures. And the road to today did not include a farewell gesture from one of America's greatest screen comedy teams.

Roger Rabbit Two:
The Toon Platoon

Since the original Roger Rabbit *was a detective comedy,* Roger Rabbit Two *was to be a military comedy—a war picture with a wacky rabbit as its star.*

Who *Framed Roger Rabbit?* was an important movie to those who love animation. It was one of the earliest in a series of events that returned American animation to a productive (and even respected) position on the entertainment landscape. When *Roger* came out, critics fell over themselves to yammer about how for the first time an animated character was just as "real" as a human character. And they were right . . . except for Bugs Bunny, Daffy and Donald Duck, Sylvester, Dumbo, and many other animation greats. What was really happening was that, having been trained by the Spielberg-era industry to expect human ciphers in the lead roles of films, they had found in Roger Rabbit an animated character equally one-dimensional. If Bob Hoskins's co-star had been Bugs Bunny, Hoskins would have had to do considerably more acting to match the rabbit's genuine multidimensionality.

Of course, the Bugs Bunny of *Space Jam* is every bit as visually overwrought and inauthentic as any character in *Roger Rabbit.* That's one of the unfortunate legacies of *Roger*—it made Bugs Bunny bankable again but only as a shell of his former self. It's ironic that the *Roger Rabbit* approach to cartoon characters embraces *visual* dimensionality but ignores *character* dimensionality. Cartoon characters of the classic sort are intrinsically flat (visually). They look their best that way, and it doesn't stop them from being "real." The interaction of human and cartoon characters in *Mary Poppins, Song of the South, You Ought to Be in Pictures,* and so many others does not become less believable because the animated characters are "flat."

Still, we can be grateful to *Roger Rabbit,* the Bakshi/Kricfalusi *Mighty Mouse,* and other important projects for helping usher in an age in which we can enjoy *King of the Hill, The Tick, South Park,* and *The Lion King.* Unfortunately, it also ushered in an era of Spielberg-mangled half-assed imitations of real cartoons. (Disney had been planning to make *Roger Rabbit* since the early eighties, but it never got off the ground until the project was given to Spielberg. As a result, Warner Bros., who owned the greatest stable of cartoon characters in entertainment history, felt they had to hand over a goodly percentage of sure-thing animated projects in order to benefit from his "touch.")

We probably would have seen more *Roger Rabbit* theatrical shorts if only Disney or Amblin' had owned Roger, but the proprietors' tussles seem to have limited our ability to enjoy the promising offshoots. Similarly lost in development hell has been the once-inevitable *Roger Rabbit* sequel. And it's a shame, because *Roger Rabbit Two: The Toon Platoon,* by Nat Mauldin, corrects many of the original's flaws and is a delightful comic alignment of man and cartoon. *The Toon Platoon* (actually a prequel) is set in 1941 and follows Roger through the days surrounding the advent of U.S. involvement in World War II. (Perhaps Spielberg may yet consider this film a kind of follow-up to *Saving Private Ryan.*)

It's important to note that during the actual World War II era, Hollywood comedies were made according to a startlingly effective formula. If Bob Hope was to be in a private eye comedy, the picture would basically be structured just like any other detective picture.

The only difference would be that it would star Bob Hope, a frightened ordinary guy, instead of someone like Alan Ladd. The familiar genre was the setup of the joke; the presence of a "regular guy" was the punch line. Nowadays, comedies are filled with unmitigated wackiness, à la the toon zanies of *Who Framed Roger Rabbit?* But without a straight element against which the craziness can be seen in perspective, there is no comedy at all. It's like having a comedy team composed of Costello and Costello. The effect is simply annoying. Well, Nat Mauldin's *Roger Rabbit Two* understands traditional comedy structure. Since the original *Roger Rabbit* was a detective comedy, *Roger Rabbit Two* was to be a military comedy—a war picture with a wacky rabbit as its star.

In *The Toon Platoon,* Roger, the adopted child of a wholesome midwestern farm couple, was left on their doorstep as a baby and didn't know he was a toon until his eighteenth birthday. With human Richie Davenport he travels west to seek his mother, in the process meeting a not-yet-glamorous Jessica Krupnick (his future wife), acquiring a Hollywood career, and going to war.

Roger among the Nazis was a capital idea, and the script contains others as well, such as hot-babe Jessica's early career as a radio actress. There are the requisite star cameos, from Wile E. Coyote to Bob Hoskins (as Eddie Valiant) and, of course, Droopy (assisting Foghorn Leghorn as a tailor taking Richie's inseam). There are "new" toon characters such as Swifty Turtle and Blackie Cat, who are used entertainingly. Even the group wackiness that is so offensive in *Space Jam* is better in a Roger Rabbit comedy, its natural home.

In the script, Jessica is kidnapped and forced to make pro-Nazi broadcasts as an unwilling Tokyo Rose–type character, so Roger and Richie must go behind enemy lines to save her. That Nat Mauldin is the son of Bill Mauldin, who created the World War II–era comic *Willie and Joe* could not have hurt him in constructing this effort. He is conversant with both the World War II milieu and the cartoon/ comic form. When Blackie Cat fouls up the villain's plans by crossing his path and causing a piano to fall on him, Mauldin shows an understanding of cartoon physics and also its appropriate use within the tale.

The best gag of all is the closing one. After their military triumph, Roger and Richie are given a Hollywood Boulevard parade. At the conclusion, Roger is finally reunited with his cartoon rabbit mother. Roger asks about his father, and the camera reveals the quintessentially posed Bugs Bunny, who asks, "Ain't I a stinker?" A hilarious revelation not unlike Darth Vader's revelation to his son Luke Skywalker.

This sums up the great strengths of this potential movie. Roger Rabbit is, in a real sense, Bugs Bunny's offspring. But more important, the cameo shows Nat Mauldin's understanding of the characters, his knowledge of when and how to use them, and his mastery of traditional comedy construction—this parting cameo is exactly like the ones in live-action films of the World War II period.

Roger Rabbit II could have been that rarity, a sequel that was better than the original. Judging from the script, it could have been the movie that the first one pretended to be. What was right with the original was maintained; what was wrong was corrected. But the project was so important that it never got made. So often, in Hollywood, projects are too important. Nothing ever seems right, and the moment passes.

Hollywood. What a maroon.

Saturday Matinee

Another feature in Saturday Matinee, *a sci-fi opus titled* Planet of the Cheap Special Effects, *developed a cult following in the entertainment industry for its acuity and hilarity.*

By the 1970s, film had gone through several golden ages of comedy. There was the golden age of Keaton, Chaplin, and Lloyd, the great silent clowns. There was a golden age of talking comedy, featuring the Marx Brothers, Mae West, W. C. Fields, and others. Many have a fondness for the era that was dominated by live-performance duos like Abbott and Costello or Martin and Lewis. And the 1970s were dominated comedically by Mel Brooks and Woody Allen.

Even though Brooks and Allen spoke assuredly to the younger generation, their comedy was clearly derived from another era. Both had worked in the live television of the 1950s and toiled upon a Borscht Belt foundation that bound them to a lengthy, primarily Jewish comedy tradition.

Simultaneous to their rising dominance in the seventies, however, there was another comedy appearing on the horizon. The *Harvard Lampoon* had spawned the *National Lampoon,* which, with its radio and theatrical spin-offs, had begun to speak to the young from within the ranks rather than from outside them. The sixties had changed the way America and its youth saw the world. The seventies were far enough along to add to that new vision some comic detachment—a loving and damning look at formative experiences viewed through an ironic prism fueled by drugs, youth, and the special qualities of the moment.

At the forefront of the comedic youth movement was Michael O'Donahue, a founder of the *National Lampoon* and a man whose dark take on pop culture was the quintessence of that comic moment. Like many from the *Lampoon* world, O'Donahue had made the move from *Lampoon* to the television program that would give its comic vision to the larger world—*Saturday Night Live* (originally NBC's *Saturday Night*). The success of *Saturday Night Live* made O'Donahue's generation bankable. When his *Lampoon* and *SNL* cohort Chevy Chase got an opportunity to segue into motion pictures, O'Donahue was asked to help provide the vehicle for the ride.

Now, as we know, in the motion picture business, the same idea is often developed and produced at the same time by more than one organization. And so it happened that during the late 1970s there was in development a film very similar in concept to what O'Donahue and Chase came up with, a Larry Gelbart project called *Movie Movie*.

Both were tributes to and evocations of a form of movie presentation by then lost to the past—a full-fledged movie show featuring cartoons, newsreels, live-action shorts, and other niceties not available in the modern era. However, Gelbart and his director, Stanley Donen, were in some respects actually of the time they celebrated, while O'Donahue and Chase clearly were not. The Gelbart/Donen project was a loving parody cum recreation; the O'Donahue/Chase project was a loving but savage balls-out parody of a time that had ended while they were still children.

Actually, while *Movie Movie* and *Saturday Matinee* both parodied the same basic concept—the full-scale movie show—the specifics of what they were parodying differed a lot. Gelbart and Donen were parodying the thirties heyday, when hard-hitting melodramas and lavish musicals were the order of the day. O'Donahue and Chase were parodying the dying days of the format, when cheap sci-fi movies were more the order of the day and full-scale movie shows were more in the province of a weekend afternoon.

Saturday Matinee was to have featured parodies of no smoking announcements, sports novelties, bouncing ball cartoons, newsreels, coming attractions, double features, a charity pitch, and a travelogue. It was filled to the brim with entertainment—all filtered through the youth generation prism of Michael O'Donahue.

In fact, O'Donahue essentially wrote the entire movie. By the time Chase was to have written his segments, the script was already substantially longer than the Hollywood average. O'Donahue steadfastly refused to cut his masterpiece, and as a result, he never got the chance to make it at all. In contrast, the makers of *Movie Movie*—seasoned Hollywood hands—excised elements of their parody due to similar length requirements. Their movie got made and was a great hit. But like the other comedies of the era, its comic roots were truly in another time.

Meanwhile, back in modern times (the seventies), Chase argued with O'Donahue in favor of compromise, but O'Donahue would not budge. O'Donahue came to blame Chase rather than his own intransigence for the movie's unfortunate demise. Chase went on to do *Foul Play,* and his movie career was truly born. (Chase's entire career died after an embarassing and short-lived talk show, but that's another story.) But *Foul Play* was yet another seventies comedy with its origins in the distant past.

Chevy Chase might have had an entirely different career if his debut picture had been *Saturday Matinee* rather than *Foul Play.* And the comedy of the seventies and eighties—not to mention that of the entire *SNL* generation—might have been off to a better, more luminous start.

The parody of *Saturday Matinee* was very acutely realized. The first of its two features, *Captain Windjammer,* had a title sequence in which a hand turned the pages of a book. The actors listed included Victor McLaglen, Patric Knowles, Douglass Dumbrille, and Alan Napier. The technical credits included the names Cedric Gibbons, Perc Westmore, and Natalie Kalmus. These are all authentic names from old movies, names that would very likely have appeared on this type of picture. This is the kind of detail that gave the *National Lampoon* its greatness during the golden period that included its high school yearbook parody.

Another feature in *Saturday Matinee,* a sci-fi opus titled *Planet of the Cheap Special Effects,* developed a cult following in the entertainment industry for its acuity and hilarity. The movie is true pop culture parody. The script for *Planet of the Cheap Special Effects* asserts that a planet has based a civilization on the 1955 Frederick's of Hollywood catalogue. The music was to be in the period style of Martin Denny, recognized in the nineties as an icon of "space-age bachelor pad" music. The film was a look back yet ahead of its time.

In *Planet of the Cheap Special Effects,* a character introduces herself by saying, "I am Voluptua, queen of the Starlos and ruler of the Lost City of Lah."

An astronaut character asks, "This is the Lost City of Lah?"

"Yes," the queen replies.

"How," the astronaut asks, "can it be the *Lost* City when we are standing in it?"

"Such questions are dangerous, Captain," replies the queen. "But we will talk later. You and your men must be tired after your long journey."

Michael O'Donahue died a few years ago. Chevy Chase's movie career expired a few years earlier. There have been parodies of some of the genres covered by *Saturday Matinee*, but nothing like the scope of *Matinee* has been attempted and no similar projects have been attempted by similar talents.

Certainly, we of the present are tired from our long journey through awful *Saturday Night Live*–inspired comedies. If only we had been able to see the trailer for *Original Shaft* (an overtly racist early version of the blaxploitation classic) or the travelogue featuring the "Kitchacorn Monkey Dance."

Grateful audiences did get to hear the song from *Saturday Matinee*'s bouncing ball cartoon. The number, called "Let's Talk Dirty to the Animals," became one of the highlights of the otherwise lackluster *Gilda Live* in 1980. And now she's gone, too. Even a potential "modern" comic golden age of the late seventies and eighties is rooted deeply in an irretrievable past. Such is the nature of time.

Say It with Music

... he nearly brought to fruition one last musical worthy of his and his studio's reputation—an extravaganza featuring the entire life's output of America's songwriter, Irving Berlin: Say It with Music.

Once upon a time, in the kingdom of Metro-Goldwyn-Mayer, there was a songwriter named Arthur Freed who wanted to be a producer. So he petitioned the great king Louis B. Mayer to allow him to produce. And though it took a while, after good Freed's contributions to a film about the wonderful *Wizard of Oz*, his fond wish was finally granted. There would, in due time, be a group of musical artisans who toiled in the land of MGM, known as the Freed Unit. And over the years, this "unit" grew and grew and became filled with the finest musical talents from among the many Hollywood kingdoms.

Judy Garland felt there was no place quite like her home in the kingdom of Metro-Goldwyn-Mayer. Gene Kelly and Fred Astaire were rivals for the position of King's Dancer, but both were good of heart and there was no ill will between them. June Allyson, Lena Horne, Keenan Wynn, Ann Miller, Ginger Rogers, Cyd Charisse, Rita Moreno, Oscar Levant, Nanette Fabray, and many others provided merriment for citizens well beyond King Mayer's domain.

Directing good Freed's players were show cobblers like Vincente Minnelli and Stanley Donen. Songs for the frolicsome larks were provided by such heralded tunesmiths as Cole Porter, Irving Berlin, and even good Freed himself (with the full participation of songsmithing partner Nacio Herb Brown).

As time went by, Hollywood's kingdoms vigorously supported World War II. But after the battles were over, the Shortsighted States of America decided to turn its war machine on the kingdoms of Hollywood themselves.

The Hollywood kingdoms had placed many playhouses throughout the Shortsighted States of America in order to present their glorious plays to as many as wished to see them. These playhouses had names like the Bijou or the Strand or Loew's Capitol or the RKO Houston, and the Hollywood kings tried to keep their play-houses filled with merriment for the benefit of good people everywhere.

But the Shortsighted States did not worship entertainment; they worshiped a god called competition. So the Shortsighted commanded that the Hollywood kings could no longer own playhouses within the Shortsighted territory. Instead, the kings could offer their plays to others' playhouses, which could present or refuse them as they wished.

Without their own playhouses, the Hollywood kings could not be certain that anyone would present their plays and players. The kings grew careful about which plays would be produced. With fewer plays to make, the kingdoms could no longer maintain their companies of players. Boxes that delivered plays into the homes of the Shortsighted brought further turmoil to the entertainment realms. Some players were forced to go into the world and act as mercenaries, to sing and dance for the highest bidders. King Mayer was toppled, and good Freed carried on under new kings while uncertainty reigned.

Eventually, even the ruby red slippers worn by Dorothy of Kansas were sold simply to pay a tattered kingdom's bills.

So, basically what I'm saying is that MGM, which made many of the greatest musicals ever presented, was by the 1970s a tattered shell of its former self—barely alive. In 1974, at the bottom of its fortunes as a moviemaking company, it released *That's Entertainment,* a tribute to the musicals that had helped make it great. One has only to remember Fred Astaire standing in front of a weathered remnant of a railroad set he had once performed on to recognize that mighty MGM had fallen far indeed.

The railroad set had been used by Astaire in *The Band Wagon,* which was produced by the amazing Arthur Freed. Now, twenty-plus years later, all that was left was decay. But one didn't have to look back two decades to find musical greatness at the studio. As recently as 1970, Arthur Freed had been toiling in his office, attempting to bring to the screen another in his series of the greatest movie musicals ever made.

Freed's MGM musicals included *Silk Stockings, An American in Paris, On the Town, Easter Parade,* and *Singing in the Rain.* Much is made of the way Disney constructs its animated musicals—working and reworking individual sequences, throwing things out that work individually but don't contribute to the whole, meticulously "constructing" the project. Well, that's how MGM's live-action musicals were made years ago. Individual musical sequences were polished over many months in preparation for their contribution to the whole.

This was possible because MGM (owned by the powerful Loew's theater chain) strove to be the best. They spent money to hire or develop the biggest talents in all movie-related fields, from set designers, to costume designers, to screenwriters, to actors, to directors. Arthur Freed's musical unit had a mandate to hire the Fred Astaires and Vincente Minnellis and Andre Previns.

But this was before movie studios were forced to get rid of their theaters. It was before studios dropped their contract players, before inexperienced businessmen making ignorant decisions became the rule rather than the exception.

Arthur Freed remained at MGM after its golden era and even managed to make successful pictures. His romantic love story *Light in the Piazza* was a critical and financial success in 1962. But Freed was a musical guy, and he wanted to make musicals.

He tried to get MGM to buy *Hello, Dolly*—and *My Fair Lady* and *Camelot*. He attempted to reactivate projects that the studio owned but never made. And though thwarted in those attempts, he nearly brought to fruition one last musical worthy of his and his studio's reputation—an extravaganza featuring the entire life's output of America's songwriter, Irving Berlin: *Say It with Music*.

Berlin, whose career had encompassed the century, was to be fully involved in this musical's creation. The penny-pinchers at MGM in 1963 were not about to fork over a truckload of money, but Berlin was willing to compromise because he trusted Arthur Freed and because he wanted as much money as possible to go into the film's budget.

MGM still had the wisdom to see the value of a Freed/Berlin musical and announced the project quickly. Ann-Margaret and Sophia Loren were to star. Arthur Laurents, who had provided the book for *Gypsy*, was to write the script.

Berlin's new songs (including "The Ten Best Undressed Women") were prepared while Laurents wrote a script in which Robert Goulet would play a ladies' man with simultaneous relationships in four different countries (Ann-Margaret/United States, Julie Andrews/England, Brigitte Bardot/France, Sophia Loren/Italy—yes, a dream come true). It's a notion that was workable, but remember, these guys were willing to throw out serious amounts of work if the project wasn't exactly right. Freed thought they could do better, so he hired Leonard Gershe to start writing anew.

Gershe worked nine months on the project, and Berlin was so enthused that he composed yet another new song, "I Used to Play by Ear." Vincente Minnelli had been participating in the development and was presumably to be the director. And Freed's longtime associate producer, Roger Edens, was lured back into the MGM fold. Bit by bit, Freed was reassembling the unit that had worked so well for so long.

Seeking innovation, Edens and Gershe constructed a "stream-of-consciousness" ballet composed of 28 songs. MGM's reaction? Its top executives kept Freed, Minnelli, and Gershe waiting for an hour and then told Freed to find another script. It would have been one thing if Freed had wanted another script, but now he was being given creative instructions from above. Still, he felt the project was important, so another script was prepared by Betty Comden and Adolph Green (coauthors of *On the Town, Bells Are Ringing, The Band Wagon,* and *Singing in the Rain,* among others) between 1963 and 1967.

Comden and Green wrote two full drafts of their script and remember that Berlin used to call to express his excitement. Their screenplay encompassed the varied eras of Berlin's music. The movie was to move between three stories, one in 1915, one in 1925, and one in 1965. Through the music and interwoven plots, we would see that though fashions may change—love remains the same.

Roger Edens left the project, but it was anticipated that the film would begin principal photography in late 1967 and include a ballet by choreographers Jerome Robbins and Bob Fosse! Fred Astaire was now to star.

Here's where desperation seems to set in.

By 1968, the *LA Times* was reporting that Julie Andrews was now to star and that Blake Edwards and Freed were to co-produce. The picture was to feature the requisite "all-star cast" as well as "one of the largest arrays of musical talent assembled for any one motion picture." It was to be a 70mm reserved seat attraction and was now to start shooting in 1969.

Suddenly in 1969, MGM was taken over by Kirk Kerkorian. It sold off its backlots, auctioned off its props, and quickly and quietly canceled *Say It with Music.* Arthur Freed gave up and left the studio in 1970. Irving Berlin was paid the money he was owed. But he told a Freed biographer, "It's much more important to me if they had made the picture. It was to be Arthur's and my swan song in motion pictures. But those 'civilians' as I call them—the guys in New York—making decisions that should have been made by Arthur Freed. They were stupid! And they lost all rights to my new songs."

Freed died in 1973. In 1974, MGM, by then only releasing a few pictures a year, had a major hit with *That's Entertainment.* The film was composed largely of Freed's work, and MGM made a bundle without having to shoot much new film. The film called Arthur Freed "The Producer Of The Most Outstanding Series Of Musicals In Motion Picture History."

Unfortunately, potentially the greatest movie musical will never be seen or heard.

The Silver Surfer

The Surfer comes to Earth and is attacked and persecuted as an alien invader. He signals Galactus, a godlike consumer of worlds, that there is energy here to sustain and feed him, then waits for Galactus's arrival.

Recently canceled by Universal Pictures was a big-budget rendition of *The Incredible Hulk* written by Jonathan Hensleigh (*Armageddon*). I chose not to include it in this book because, by most accounts, the script wasn't very good. But there were approximately ten previous drafts by a writer named John Turman that were right on the money. Harry Knowles, on his "Ain't It Cool News" *Web site, wrote: "If I could wave a wand, this is the one I would choose to go with. It is not camp, it is loyal to the material, and it DID NOT FEEL DATED."*

There is a reason for this. Turman, having grown up with the characters, feels a loyalty to them and believes in them:

> *The problem with "comic book" films is that they will not make them without the insurance of a top marketable director and his "vision." Most of the executives and producers involved in these projects are trying to make a buck, market a product. They are not fans, many of them have spent little or no time with the genre as kids, reading*

pulps, sci-fi or comics. They are businessmen who think they have found an angle they can market. There is a reason the best comic book films (Terminator I & II, Indiana Jones, RoboCop) are not based on comic books. When it is based on an actual comic book, executives and producers have an awareness of it as a "comic book" project and they talk about it differently, they think different rules of character and believability apply, or don't apply at all. "It's only a comic book, it doesn't have to make sense." Villains can just be crazy or evil. Action and character is unmotivated. But this is wrong and results in films like Judge Dredd, Tank Girl, recent Batmans and others.

Though he was bumped from *The Hulk* by a hotter (and, in this case, lesser) writer, Turman generated enough heat that he was offered a chance to script another major comic book film—*The Silver Surfer*. He approached his new challenge with typical enthusiasm.

The screenwriter saw the Surfer saga as "essentially a variation on the Christ myth. A messiah story about the arrival of a (somewhat absurdist) divine figure (the Surfer) presaging the arrival of a god-like figure (Galactus), who in this case is not benevolent, but an indifferent god, whose arrival signals our apocalypse." Turman decided to deal directly with the absurdity of a silver man on a surfboard, making one of the lead characters "a SETI researcher who has spent his career debunking UFOs and aliens and doesn't believe they exist. Now he is faced with a real alien and it's not a little green man with big eyes. It's a silver man on a surfboard. It's ridiculous. But what do you do when confronted with the ridiculous?"

The Surfer comes to Earth and is attacked and persecuted as an alien invader. He signals Galactus, a godlike consumer of worlds, that there is energy here to sustain and feed him, then waits for Galactus's arrival. As do we.

In the meantime, however, the Surfer experiences the nature of humanity and finds himself connecting with the people of our planet.

By the time Galactus arrives, the Surfer considers the humans his friends. But how do you stop an all-powerful god?

The secret to thwarting Galactus's deadly plans lies in Turman's musing, *What if we are the only world in the universe that has music or art?* In the midst of Galactus's reduction of all life on Earth to energy that he can feed on, music is inadvertently played over a loudspeaker system, and the god figure takes notice of it. Suddenly the life-forms he had regarded as inconsequential are perplexing to him. Galactus has never experienced music before. It is something Galactus does not understand, and he *will not* destroy that which he does not understand. At least not on this trip. This odd human notion of art, combined with the Surfer's willingness to sacrifice his own life for the new world he cares about, persuades Galactus to desist.

"It was not a conventional movie in that the villain is defeated or destroyed," explains Turman. "It felt false to destroy or defeat something as all-powerful as Galactus. What mattered is that our world gets another chance.

"I had to argue for the inclusion of Galactus," reveals Turman. "You cannot tell the story of the Silver Surfer without him. The producers were at first adamant that Galactus not be in the story. In the early drafts, I included him as an alien presence, but I gradually wore them down and won them over and Galactus was included. It was enough of a challenge to tell the origin of the Surfer and the defeat of Galactus without including the Fantastic Four and the Ultimate Nullifier, which were the basis of the origin story in the comic books.

"The key to Galactus was his scale," continued Turman. "He was conceived as huge, a mother ship in human form, a universe of complexity in every inch—this was well before *Independence Day,* but visualize the detail in those ships given an immense humanoid shape."

Here we have a writer who wants to create film versions of comic heroes that comic book fans will actually recognize and is thwarted at every turn. On *The Hulk,* he was bumped by another writer; then the film was canceled. *The Silver Surfer* movie is in limbo as well.

What do you expect from Constantin Films, the company that made a cheapo *Fantastic Four* movie just to hold onto the rights—then sat on the completed film in exchange for cash? Turman, though he has had some of his screenwriting produced, nevertheless feels like that unique Hollywood phenomenon—the successful screenwriter whose movies don't get made.

Disheartened by some aspects of his experiences, Turman has decided to stay away from "comic book" films for a while. But he is a true believer in the Marvel sense, and he recently agreed to tackle *Buck Rogers* for the good folks over at Disney. If he gets even some of his ideas about the integrity for pulp characters through the development process, we will all be the richer.

Turman, however, has no illusions about the way these things work out. And he cares so passionately about the need for these things to be done right that it matters not whether he provides the vehicle. Says the writer, "The only chance for satisfying 'comic book' films lies with the few directors who understand them, take them seriously, and have the power to convince a studio." He cites James Cameron as a man who has the requisite mixture of understanding and power. Even if Turman can't get his authentic comic visions to the screen, he still wants to see their like. It isn't too much to ask that so-called adaptations be done right.

Says Turman, "I hope Cameron makes *Spider-Man*."

Well, we'll see.

Singing Out Loud

Rob Reiner has been quoted as saying, "For a film that wasn't made it was one of the greatest creative experiences I ever had."

There is little doubt that Stephen Sondheim is the most important writer in American musical theater. The theme-parking of Broadway has spelled disaster for the traditional Broadway musical that had developed until the eighties. An Andrew Lloyd Webber show is generally appreciated for its overall production rather than its value as musical theater. There used to be a joke about a failed musical that went something like, "The audience left the theater humming the scenery." To a great extent that is what we have now—shows that value sets over songs.

Sondheim in the midst of this bombast (the Broadway equivalent of the movies' takeover by big-budget special effects) has been steadfast in his devotion to musicals with an appropriate emphasis on music. He's not retro. On the contrary, his shows push the envelope of what can be done in a musical. But they're not about the envelope; they're about its content.

Sweeney Todd, Sunday in the Park with George, Follies, A Little Night Music . . . these are names to be conjured with, and they're all Stephen

Sondheim shows. Sondheim has continued the development of the musical as a theatrical form in which songs move the story forward and express the characters' natures and needs. And he's done this without sacrificing the songs themselves, which are musical and compelling on their own. You need only listen to a recording of *"Send in the Clowns,"* be it by Judy Collins, Sinatra, or the original cast, to know that Sondheim is truly a great songwriter.

Ironically, on his first shows, Sondheim was not a musical composer at all. He was a lyricist, supplying the words for Leonard Bernstein's music in *West Side Story*

Director Rob Reiner regretted never being able to make *Singing Out Loud.*

and Jule Styne's in *Gypsy.* (Before that, Sondheim wrote episodes of TV's *Topper.*) His lyrics for others' music are awesome achievements on their own, but beginning with *A Funny Thing Happened on the Way to the Forum* Sondheim has supplied both music and lyrics to all his shows.

After *Forum,* which was instigated by Larry Gelbart and Burt Shevelove, came the development of what can be called Sondheim shows. Despite the assistance of brilliant collaborators like George Furth and James Lapine, who supplied the nonmusical "books" for Sondheim's shows, increasingly, these were his pieces to the core.

Though he has not by any means abandoned the theater, Sondheim has not been uninterested in film. He is reported to have said, "Film musicals, as opposed to stage musicals, are a territory that fascinates me, because film is a reportorial medium and theater is a poetic medium. I've rarely seen musicals work on film, musicals that tell stories and explore character, and I'd like to have a go at solving that problem."

Well, toward that end, Sondheim once asked screenwriter and author William Goldman whether Goldman thought Sondheim's *Company* (which starred film actor Dean Jones) would make a good movie.

Goldman reportedly thought that "*Company* is one of those shows, along with *Gypsy* and *Pal Joey*, that I think of as the greatest, quintessential, most beloved musicals." He continued, "I remember seeing *Company* five times and I loved it, and I had a huge . . . problem, which was that the main character's gay but they don't talk about it. Hal [Prince, the frequent Sondheim director], George [Furth] and Steve all think it's about a guy with a commitment problem."

Goldman was enthusiastic about the opportunity to address the show's weakness: "Anyway, I loved the show. And I figured out a way to change it, keep the score, but give it some narrative."

Sounds great, huh? Well, of course, they didn't do it. Sondheim had dinner with Herbert Ross, the director of *Play It Again, Sam, Footloose,* and *The Turning Point,* among other films. Ross apparently told Sondheim that since the movie couldn't possibly be better than the show, he oughtn't do it. And so he didn't. Goldman was struck by the level of Sondheim's vulnerability. (In Goldman's account of the event, he refers to the director—presumably to be dismissive— as "the choreographer, Herb Ross." Goldman is not being inaccurate, merely incomplete.)

Some time after this, around 1990, Rob Reiner called Goldman (the two have been frequent collaborators) and told him that he had an idea for a movie musical. *Singing Out Loud* was to be about a movie musical in trouble. Expecting nothing, Goldman called Sondheim. He was astonished to discover that Sondheim was extremely interested.

Sondheim jumped into the collaboration with the same intensity that characterized his work in the theater. There have been some movie adaptations of Sondheim's shows, but this would have been the first "Sondheim movie."

As an example of just how intense his creative involvement was— one day, Rob Reiner, his partner, William Goldman, and Sondheim were hashing out the picture. There was to be a scene in a recording studio wherein the heroine would try to sing a song but find herself lacking confidence and unable to complete her task. It was conceived as a significant sequence, intended to take place over eight to ten continuous minutes of film. Apparently, Sondheim said, "I can try that."

Goldman reported, "Wow, that's a lot of work to do. And he did it. It's a great, great scene." (And this comment from the screenwriter of *Butch Cassidy and the Sundance Kid* and *All the President's Men*.) Goldman continued, "Most guys would say, 'I can write the song and you guys make the book work.' But Steve was willing to get in and do the whole thing."

At about this time, however, another musical came out and was a big failure. As usual, the money people believed that audiences vote on genre, rather than individual pictures. (These knuckleheads believe that if the public doesn't want to see a bad or badly marketed movie that just happens to be a musical [or Western or whatever], it's because it's a musical [or Western or whatever] and not because it was badly made or sold.) The projected $50 million budget of the Sondheim/Goldman/Reiner *Singing Out Loud* became a frightening figure to the money men, and the project was canceled.

Forget the fact that Rob Reiner, one of America's top directors, was involved. Ignore the presence of William Goldman, one of the best screenwriters of all time. This was to be an original movie musical by the greatest artist in the American musical theater.

Rob Reiner has been quoted as saying, "For a film that wasn't made it was one of the greatest creative experiences I ever had."

Yet they didn't make *Singing Out Loud*. For cryin' out loud . . .

Something's Gotta Give

Marilyn even confidently performed Hollywood's first modern-era nude scene, a naked swim sequence . . .

Marilyn Monroe's performance in *Something's Gotta Give* would have catapulted her to Oscar-caliber status as an actress. Unfortunately, she died tragically during the production.

"When an irresistible force such as you," goes the old song lyric, "meets an old immovable object like me. . . . Somethin's gotta give, somethin's gotta give—somethin's gotta give!"

Well, when the irresistible force is Marilyn Monroe and the immovable object is the vast 20th Century-Fox studio, the something that's gotta give is likely to be the vulnerable Monroe. And that's just what happened during the 1962 production of the appropriately titled *Something's Gotta Give*.

There should be little doubt that *Something's Gotta Give* is one of the great unmade films. Though the simple story had been used before (the Cary Grant/Irene Dunne starrer *My Favorite Wife*) and though it would be used again, the script written by Nunnally Johnson and rewritten by Walter Bernstein, there was something special about this production that made it a "must-see movie." And that something is Marilyn Monroe.

"But," you say—proudly exercising your native skepticism— "Marilyn Monroe was in a lot of pictures. If she's the only reason this picture makes the cut, maybe it shouldn't make it at all." "Pshaw!" I say in return, This is not just any Marilyn Monroe. This is a Marilyn Monroe who had come through the experience of making John Huston's *The Misfits*. This is a Marilyn Monroe well on her way into maturing into a great actress. This is a sixties Marilyn—not all torpedo-bosomed and unapproachable. This Marilyn has a natural, flowing sensuality, with long, loose hair and an air of sublime reality. This Marilyn Monroe is the Kennedy-era Monroe. Indeed, she flew to New York to sing "Happy Birthday, Mr. President" during production of the film. I don't care if you've seen other Marilyn Monroe movies; you never saw this Marilyn Monroe movie!

The Marilyn Monroe of whom I'm speaking didn't even want to make *Something's Gotta Give*. She was forced into it by the terms of her Fox contract. Monroe really wanted to continue playing more significant roles, but ironically, her ability to do so successfully is one of the reasons *Something's Gotta Give* promised to be such an awesome picture. The surviving footage demonstrates that the combination of the time (the sixties), Monroe's personal growth, and the traditional Hollywood entertainment package that Fox was putting them into formed a glorious hybrid that hasn't been seen since—a luminescent golden age Hollywood-style movie made after the dawn of the sixties without seeming irrelevant or old-fashioned. That's why I say that Monroe is the key element of the picture's greatness—as well as notable cast members such as comedy greats Wally Cox and Phil Silvers.

This was the era of the Rat Pack, with whom Marilyn was known to consort. Her leading man in his definitive moment in time was Dean Martin. The storyline of the film goes that Marilyn, after an accident at sea, had been stranded on an island for years. When she finally gets back home, her husband (Dean), who presumed she was dead, has just married another woman (played by Cyd Charisse, a relic from the old world of the 1950s and thus destined to lose.)

It's a familiar story, but it's what Monroe did with it that's important. Marilyn went so far as to collaborate on the script of the picture, so assured had her star-as-auteur instincts become. Dean Martin even pronounced her work on the story "first rate."

Marilyn even confidently performed Hollywood's first modern-era nude scene, a naked swim sequence supervised by Lawrence Schiller, who was then a top magazine photographer but has since directed such projects as *The Executioner's Song.*

Unfortunately, Marilyn was saddled not only with her own well-publicized vulnerabilities but also with a studio that was in turmoil and a director with whom she was incompatible.

Director George Cukor, with whom she had previously made *Let's Make Love* (and who had been known for decades as a "woman's director"), said, "I have come to loathe Marilyn Monroe. She is a spoiled, pampered superstar and represents all that is bad about Hollywood today." Meanwhile, the studio was hemorrhaging money on the out-of-control epic *Cleopatra* and was having trouble meeting its financial obligations. Fox sold its vast studio lot to developers who were to build what is now Century City next to the shrunken studio remains. Eventually, with Fox hamstrung by survival issues that had nothing to do with Marilyn Monroe, the studio shut down production and chose Marilyn as the fall gal.

For decades, the conventional wisdom has been that Marilyn was a shambles on the set and that the picture just could not have been completed with her in that state. But though she had a couple of crises during production, her work on the picture was exemplary. Unfortunately, no one knew this for decades, until a Fox news producer found the reels of Marilyn's golden work in a storage facility in a Kansas salt mine.

An exhaustive review of the footage indicated that she made only four inconsequential mistakes during all the weeks of shooting. In addition, she proved extremely adept at replicating her performance take after take after take. The man who edited the rough cut during production said, "I don't remember a major mistake on the film I edited. . . . Marilyn Monroe never looked or acted better. . . . I had seen her in fairly bad shape on *Let's Make Love,* but there was none of that there."

Of course this vindication comes far too late to benefit Monroe herself. She died mere months later under mysterious circumstances that only made the inaccurate rumors of her "failure" on *Something's Gotta Give* seem more believable. Unfortunately, as Elton John sang, the candle burned out long before the legend ever did.

Star Trek VI: Starfleet Academy

Imagine if you will . . . a return to red, blue, and beige shirts, sexy female yeomen in short skirts and shiny black go-go boots, and a young, ambitious James Tiberius Kirk impatiently awaiting word as to whether he has been accepted by Starfleet Academy.

Sometimes an idea is so good, it manages to tick people off but good. One such idea was the plan Harve Bennett had for *Star Trek VI*—a film that was intended to be called *Star Trek: Starfleet Academy*.

After the triumph of 1986's *Star Trek IV: The Voyage Home*, everything in the *Star Trek* universe underwent significant change. Paramount was moved to mount *Star Trek: The Next Generation*, a brand-new Star Trek television series featuring an entirely new cast of characters and set in the twenty-fourth century. It premiered in 1987 and was an immediate success. Suddenly there were other major players in the *Trek* mythos and Kirk, Spock, and their thespian masters no longer had the same kind of leverage with the muckety-mucks that they had before. (Me, I'm a fan of the classic *Trek* and all its clichés. The dynamic triumvirate of Kirk, Spock, and McCoy just cannot be repeated.)

In addition, Gene Roddenberry, having been shoved aside during the production of the Harve Bennett–produced movies, had created a second successful *Star Trek* from scratch. Roddenberry was once again the acknowledged master. He had caught "lightning in a bottle" for the second time. Compared to that, it probably seemed Harve Bennett was just coloring by the numbers.

Regardless, inertia is a potent force and momentum is a hard thing to flag, so in 1989 another *Star Trek* movie was produced featuring the original cast under Harve Bennett's auspices. After all, when your last effort was a blockbuster like *The Voyage Home,* you don't shift gears for any reason.

OK—maybe you shift gears for one reason. Maybe your star, William Shatner, feels it's *his* turn to direct because your other star, Leonard Nimoy, has done it twice before. And maybe your last movie was so successful that you figure, *What the hell, we're gigantic now. He can't hurt us too much. And since I can't put him off much longer I might as well let him do it now.*

And maybe that movie is not such a big success. Maybe it's not the director's fault, but meanwhile, maybe Gene Roddenberry has created a new version of the series from scratch and you couldn't even score big-time with the original cast.

Well, maybe you think it's time to find your own new cast. Perhaps there's a way you can start over with the familiar characters so that they will be young again—played by a whole new gang of actors over whom you have complete, unmitigated control. Maybe the way that would happen would be to make a film called *Starfleet Academy.*

And that's just what Harve Bennett was going to do—reinvigorate the franchise by telling a story set at the Starfleet Academy during the days when Kirk and Spock were naive, wide-eyed students.

Young Dr. McCoy was also to be a student at the academy, and Montgomery Scott was a professor of engineering. The film was to be framed by Shatner, as the older Kirk, telling the story of the maiden voyage of the *Enterprise* to a group of latter-day academy cadets. Leonard Nimoy was also to have made an appearance.

Harve Bennett felt that this story structure was "brilliant" because "it had reinvolved Bill and Leonard as a framework, and . . . it clearly said to the audience, 'Don't worry, we're not killing the franchise, we're simply stopping to remember.' "

This was Bennett's ace in the hole. Because of the structure of the film, if the public demanded it, he could easily go back to the original cast members for *Star Trek VII*.

Paramount boss Frank Mancuso is reported to have said, "This is a great script. We're going to make this movie." However, he followed that with, "But first we want you to make a conventional *Star Trek* movie with the original cast."

Mancuso's decision was more or less inevitable. For one thing, the will of the fans had been conjured. George Takei, for instance, appealed to the fans at conventions every weekend for three months in an effort to keep a new cast from replacing his confederates. Oh, my.

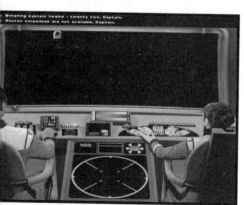

Star Trek: Starfleet Academy would have taken a young Kirk, Spock, and McCoy on their first adventure together. These images are from the computer game from Interplay of the same name.

In addition, Gene Roddenberry, the so-called Great Bird of the Galaxy, was not pleased with Bennett's plans. According to William Shatner, Roddenberry was "lobbying against the film at every turn," spreading the word that the film was to be modeled after the *Police Academy* series. He believed that Bennett was ignoring the importance of the actors to the success of the *Trek* characters. According to Walter Koenig, however, Roddenberry didn't care that the parts were being recast. He just felt he should be the one to recast them.

It's ironic that Roddenberry had complained about Bennett's idea, because back before the first *Trek* picture was made he himself had suggested a Starfleet Academy idea—kind of a prequel of sorts or a *Kirk, Spock, and McCoy: The Early Days*. At that time, however, the original cast were deemed young enough to play earlier incarnations of themselves. (Walter Koenig, in fact, was deemed too young, since his character would have been a child when others were attending the academy. Koenig would have played a cameo as Chekov's father.)

Even during Roddenberry's relative "exile" from original cast projects, the team seemed to be clinging strongly to his concepts. For example, *Star Trek V*'s "God" premise had also been one of Roddenberry's early movie ideas. As Roddenberry associate Richard Arnold later told William Shatner, "This was a story that [Roddenberry] wanted to tell and that he hadn't been allowed to."

This pressure from all sides, plus the fact of the series's upcoming twenty-fifth anniversary, doomed the academy idea for the time being, and Bennett left the studio. (According to some sources, he was fired.) Chairman of the board Martin Davis had personally insisted that the next *Trek* film feature the original cast. Bennett later reported, "For the first time in my life I drank excessively. I don't mind saying that I drank a lot. That's the truth, and thank God I got over that. . . . I was terribly hurt."

At any rate, the *Starfleet Academy* idea was never produced as a film. (There is, however, a Starfleet Academy CD-ROM game featuring appearances by Shatner, Koenig, and Takei.) The sixth *Star Trek* picture was ultimately the Leonard Nimoy–produced, Nick Meyer–directed *Star Trek VI: The Undiscovered Country*.

Starfleet Academy as envisioned by Harve Bennett now resides amid the dust of the unproduced story pile over at Paramount. But the script remains a great untold *Trek* tale. Imagine if you will . . . a return to red, blue, and beige shirts, sexy female yeomen in short skirts and shiny black go-go boots, and a young, ambitious James Tiberius Kirk impatiently awaiting word as to whether he has been accepted by Starfleet Academy. Once accepted, the Iowa lad meets his classmates, including the Vulcan, Spock, who was defying his father by being there, and McCoy, who had to that point been caring for his dying father. Spock is the first alien to attend the academy and is thought of by his classmates in much the same way that early settlers thought of Indians—with distrust by all except for Kirk. Kirk and Spock would not have hit it off immediately; indeed, they would have been rivals. Kirk, however, would stand up for Spock against troubling racial taunts and thus would begin their longtime friendship.

Kirk would have faced repercussions for this from fellow cadets who were being manipulated by a racist demagogue operating from space itself. Kirk then meets his first great love—indeed, the film was to have explained why Kirk was unable to commit to love thereafter. The cadets of course, though untested, would find themselves the only hope of a desperate world.

And at the conclusion Kirk and Spock were to have parted, not knowing if they would ever see each other again.

In the "modern" story, we would ultimately have found Shatner as the now-older Kirk at the grave site of his lost love. Spock would have come looking for his friend at the cemetery. "I have deep feelings," Kirk would have told his comrade. "You wouldn't understand."

"Captain," Nimoy as Spock would have said, "I might not have feelings, but I have memories. Beam us up, Scotty."

According to Bennett, the film was to have explained why Kirk and Spock were "joined so irrevocably at the hip" and why Bones is always "saying, 'No, no!' all the time."

The script itself is moving. It's unfortunate that studio meddling, actors' egos, and petty Hollywood power plays have deprived us of what could have been the greatest *Star Trek* tale of all. However, as computer technology improves and young filmmakers using high-powered software inch ever closer to acurately re-creating humans on screen, we may yet see new *Trek* adventures with a new cast of young "digital" actors. Think of the possibilities. . . .

Statical Planets

Statical Planets was to be an intentionally funny reiteration of the sort of B movies that were featured on Mystery Science Theater 3000.

There is a hierarchy among stand-up comedians, and toward the bottom, near ventriloquists and jugglers, are the "prop comics." "Straight" stand-ups (this term is not meant in a sexual way—there are gay straight stand-ups) look down upon their prop-oriented brethren as cheap exploitationists who can't think of anything funny to say. (Think Gallagher, for example. You do remember Gallagher, don't you?) On the other hand, during the first half of the eighties there was a comedian named Joel Hodgson whose act was as prop-oriented as you could get, yet nobody looked down on him.

The reason for the fabled "Hodgson Exemption" was simple: Hodgson was damn funny! I don't mean his act was funny; I mean *he* was funny. His toys weren't earning his laughs; he was. He was a "true comic," who happened to think in terms of objects instead of just words.

He was quite successful. Even Jerry Seinfeld, the quintessential talking comic, went to Hodgson when he needed a collaborator for a cable special. Joel did *Letterman* successfully and seemed to be on his way. Then he left stand-up . . . voluntarily.

He was done.

Other guys would've killed for a fraction of what Joel was achieving, but he would have none of it. He abandoned the entertainment capitals to return to his home turf in Minnesota. When a friend of mine saw him a few years later and asked him what he was doing, he replied, "I make robots from found objects."

Huh?

But those robots or their descendants turned out to be Crow and the other magical constructs that populated Hodgson's *Mystery Science Theater 3000*.

MST3K, as it's known, debuted on a UHF station in the Minneapolis area in 1988 as a creative way of showing the station's movies. The witty commentary and whimsical framing stories were so delightful that in 1989 the series moved to cable's fledgling Comedy Channel (later to be merged into Comedy Central).

And so Joel was into the second volume of his show biz career. He eventually left *MST3K*, though his creation continued without him (first on Comedy Central and then on the Sci-Fi Channel). He moved back to Los Angeles and divided his time between mainstream projects and personal conceits. He co-wrote *Honey, We Shrunk Ourselves* and was a magic consultant for *Sabrina, the Teenage Witch*, but he also produced an innovative pilot, *The TV Wheel*, and attempted the production of a motion picture called *Statical Planets*.

Statical Planets was to be an intentionally funny reiteration of the sort of B movies that were featured on *Mystery Science Theater 3000*. It was to have been in black and white and to have featured the magic of "Static-A-Matic," Joel's loving tribute to the William Castle gimmicks of the fifties.

Where Castle had electrified theater seats during showings of his *The Tingler*, Joel would similarly allow audiences to experience the astonishing sensation of static electricity. Joel intended to distribute the picture unconventionally, touring with it to colleges and similar venues. He even shot a trailer designed to raise the funds necessary to make the film.

The trailer features Morwenna Banks, Melissa Samuels, the ubiquitous Nick Bakay, Paul Feig, Steve Bannos, John Carney, and (from *MST3K*) Frank Conniff. Conniff has said, "It actually had a very complicated plot." Elements of the plot are easily gleaned from the Internet "trading cards" Joel devised to promote the picture. The Middle-American Hodgson posits that an easy way to make homes look good is what people really want. The film asserts that they will use such a technique to the point of self-destruction, like a monkey with an orgasm button:

> *Developed by renegade Gizmocrat Adrian Topaz. The Electron Scaffolding was a commercially available cloaking device that could convince great columns of electrons and protons into beautifying the exteriors of homes. It quickly became the most popular electronic device in the Alternaverse—out-selling the television 5-to-1. Its use, mis-use and abuse by lazy fix-er-up-ers is cited as the reason for overriding the electro-radio bandwidth and breaking electricity forever.*

The cards go on to say: "Electricity didn't function anymore—but it wasn't gone. It had mutated into a useless, annoying strain of static electricity that clung to everything and everybody. A person in the Alternaverse can receive as many as 100 shocks a day, depending on what kind of carpeting you have."

When a character in the film received a shock, the audience was expected to receive one as well, through the magic of "Static-A-Matic." Of course, "Static-A-Matic," utilizing the ever-astonishing phenomenon of static electricity, required audience participation in order to work. It was explained: "Static-A-Matic" is a story device that does what static electricity does in your own home, but on a much larger scale. "Static-A-Matic" is an interactive event and only with your cooperation *re-creates the powerful illusion of static electricity on the screen, in the theater and all around you.*

If for any reason you are uncomfortable with the proximity of the machinery to your person or its triggering system you can waive your direct participation with the Static-A-Matic process and enjoy the movie in total safety—static free.

I saw the trailer several times in rooms filled with people, and when the refrain "Static-A-Matic, Static-A-Matic . . ." issued from the screen, the crowd squealed with delight despite the absence of any actual apparatus in the area. Audiences love the elements of movie gimmicks, and *Statical Planets* plays into that love.

Joel's promotional materials claim the film utilized a method called the Hodgson Backscreen 96 process. They explain:

It is projected that 90 percent of Statical Planets *filmed in Static-A-Matic will be filmed using the Hodgson Backscreen 96 process. The Hodgson Backscreen 96 is a method of projecting a background image onto a screen, hence the name* backscreen, *and was developed by Jim and Joel Hodgson. The Hodgson brothers cobbled the first backscreen together using some of the newest imaging technology and a World War II overhead projector. Rearscreen or rear-projection is the traditional method by which this process is usually accomplished, however it proved too costly for the low budget confines of* Statical Planets, *so the efficient Hodgson Backscreen 96 was born.*

The project was filled with amazing notions. Animals had their own political party (and were toilet trained). The most popular beverage before the electricity broke was "anti-cola." Frank Conniff was to play an entire army—"The Frank 300 Army"—and would have also played a king.

Unfortunately, financing issues prevented further production beyond the making of the trailer. Joel, true to character, has moved on to other interests and pursuits. (One of his enterprises is a collaboration with Ernie Kovacs's heirs on how best to perpetuate the Kovacs creative legacy.) Working outside the system and according to his own designs has allowed Joel Hodgson to develop a unique comic outlook and persona, but, sadly, it did not facilitate the production of the potentially wondrous *Statical Planets*.

Swirlee

A gangster movie about a godfather made of ice cream?

Before Tarantino reintroduced moviegoers to gangsters, mafiosi, and Bible-quoting tough guys, James Lorinz envisioned a different take on the gangster genre. "Swirlee is torn between being a man and being something that he's not," says Lorinz. "He wants to experience the things that other men feel, like making love to a woman."

One minor problem stands in his way—Swirlee is made of ice cream. Yep, ice cream. Imagine a gritty crime drama, à la Scorsese's *Mean Streets,* in which the lead character has a head shaped like a delicious creamy swirl. Swirlee is like *GoodFellas* meets *The Elephant Man* by way of *Edward Scissorhands.*

This abandoned project was the brainchild of James Lorinz, a former student at New York's School of Visual Arts, who is a twisted gent to be sure. Witness Lorinz's acting performances in films like *Street Trash* (as the wisecracking doorman) and *Frankenhooker* (as the young mad scientist).

Swirlee first sprang to life in the confines of Lorinz's skull when he was a film student:

I had a vision of this ice cream guy lying in a bathtub, half melted, with his brain throbbing. At the time, I was greatly influenced by the film Raging Bull, *and I wanted to make something in that vein of realism. I wanted to do a story about a guy who wasn't totally human, but I would make the audience accept him through the urbane relationships he has with the various characters. I would put in elements of exploitation that would appeal to distributors (making it a gangster picture with violence and sex), but I would retain the very human story about this poor deformed guy. In other words, if I can get the audience to accept the image of the ice cream cone within five minutes, and to understand the kind of story it's going to be, then it won't be a gimmick, and the story will play out as a drama, which makes it funny.*

The ice cream man has certainly bent this gent's head. The idea lay dormant for a few years (James never got around to finishing his student film) and was reborn after he finished acting in a television sitcom: "I took some money and shot a short trailer and some rough-cut footage." In 1989, Lorinz invested $10,000 of his own money in shooting test footage. (This footage, a 2-minute trailer and a 15-minute rough cut, is all that exists of the project.) The footage starred Lorinz's old pal David Caruso (of *NYPD Blue* butt-flashing fame), character actor Tony Darrow, and Lorinz himself as the title character.

"The Swirlee makeup took about two hours to put on in the morning and an hour to take it off, so it cut into the shooting time. With the makeup on it was like directing underwater!" says Lorinz.

Gangsters with names like Don Tofutti, Don Sorbet, and Don Gelato run a shifty artificial ice cream company that helped put Swirlee out of business. "Swirlee is all washed up," says Lorinz. "He's a very weak character. It's a terrific role to play as an actor. He starts out being sort of like Fredo in *The Godfather,* then he becomes successful and can't handle it, so he becomes quite ugly. By the end of the film, he redeems himself."

The scenes in the test footage succeed wonderfully in that they are compelling and believable, like any good drama. The ridiculousness of the idea of a frozen-headed crime lord is quickly forgotten in the scenes between Lorinz and Caruso. Their dramatic exchanges result in a tearful suicide attempt in which Swirlee takes a warm bath. (Aw, he just wants to be warm inside, but he can't because he'll melt. The irony!)

James Lorinz as the title character from *Swirlee*, a gritty New York crime drama about a cold-hearted mobster made of ice cream.

"Swirlee doesn't know what it's like to be warm," says Lorinz. "He's fed up with being cold all the time. He doesn't want to be who he is! Imagine, a guy who's a human ice cream cone at OTB placing bets . . . totally straight, maybe coughing on a cigarette. It's a very interesting kind of funny. It's not him slipping on a banana peel and going, 'Whoaaa!' I picked Rocko Simonelli to write the screenplay because I knew he could keep the concept in reality."

Swirlee screenplay author Rocko Simonelli makes no bones about it . . . this is not being played for laughs: "There are no jokes. It's not played as a comedy. Once you start laying jokes on top of this, it's over-kill! When we started talking about doing this idea as a feature length screenplay, we had to decide what direction we were going to take. My approach was, *How would I feel if I was made out of ice cream?*"

It was Rocko's job to give the concept a logical basis so that the dramatic angle made sense. And so the Swirlee mythos was born. "Swirlee is a Nodropinem baby," says Rocko. "It's something akin to the thalidomide babies: the scandal of the early 1960s. Women were

taking this antimorning sickness
drug, and their kids were being
born with flippers, fins, and all
kinds of deformities. Nodropinem
is an antimiscarriage drug that
Swirlee's mother was taking and it
works fine, except if the woman
eats one specific kind of food in
excess during her pregnancy,
whatever her craving is, the baby
is born with its body manifesting

the characteristics of that particular type of food. There's a whole
sequence in the film in the Nodropinem ward with a series of Nodropinem babies. A pizza baby. A pickle baby. You understand? Swirlee is a human being, but he is ice cream."

Lorinz then teamed up with
producer Roy Frumkes, whose
two major contributions to indie
film have been the documentary
Document of the Dead (1990), a
chronicle on the making of George
Romero's independent masterpiece
Dawn of the Dead (1979), and
Street Trash (1987), the hard-to-de-
scribe, love-it-or-loathe-it, genre-
unto-itself film written and produced by Frumkes.

"I often used the analogy of *Dick Tracy* when I talked to investors,"
says Frumkes. "Only this is *Dick Tracy* meets *Mean Streets*. *Dick Tracy*
and *Edward Scissorhands* were films that were played somewhat over
the top. It's played really straight. The gag exists and permeates within
it, but only because of what Swirlee is."

Each "never-made" film has unique reasons for landing in limbo.
Swirlee's enemy came in the form of unimaginative studio heads.

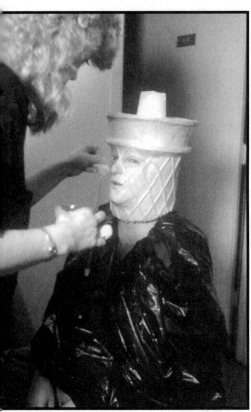

James Lorinz goes through the grueling process of applying make-up.

"It was a hard concept to sell," says Roy. "Money people and studios feel the film should be for kids, that the humor should be on a child's level."

Lorinz adds, "I'm willing to compromise within reason. I mean, if somebody understands the concept, then you can talk. One company was very hot on the idea, but they had objections to the scene where Swirlee tries to commit suicide by lying in a tub of hot water. It's a pivotal scene in the movie, but they had a lot of trouble with that."

"They wanted to do it very one-dimensionally, very silly. Very much a live-action *Frosty the Snowman*," says Simonelli. "When you tell somebody about our idea, the usual reaction is, 'Oh, very cute little one-joke idea,' and that's how they want to make it. We want to be three-dimensional. You'll get your laughs. Relax. Let the story happen."

"We wanted to retain our creative license. Many of the people we spoke to had trouble with the dark, downbeat nature of the concept," Frumkes states. "There is an unspoken war between the distributors and the artists. Absolutely! A to-the-death, horns-locking war. They disguise it by saying that they're doing market research. What they really want to do is emasculate us."

Currently *Swirlee* remains unproduced, but James has never given up on the project. He feels that the resurgence in crime dramas only makes *Swirlee* more bankable, plus the fact that ice cream seems to

still be a hit among people everywhere. James Lorinz relocated to
Burbank, California, where he
makes money on the odd acting
job, Roy Frumkes teaches film at
New York's School of Visual Arts,
and David Caruso's film career
never quite got off the ground. The
creative trio have gone their separate ways waiting for the day to
make this film. Besides a segment
on *Hard Copy* that featured the
Swirlee footage starring David Ca-

James Lorinz wrote, starred, and directed the test footage, which is all
that exists of *Swirlee*.

ruso, and the odd bootleg tape, the footage has only been seen by a
few lucky souls.

That's Life

It was described as a "senior citizen's Animal House" and was to star Academy Award winner Red Buttons, Harold and Maude's Ruth Gordon, Yiddish theater veteran Molly Picon, and other notable oldsters.

Imagine you were a man who became a movie star by the time he was in his early twenties. Imagine further that by the time you reached your midthirties you were also a writer and director—and your movies made lots of money. In some quarters, namely France, you were even proclaimed a genius!

Now imagine you've become addicted to pills and your work begins to suffer. You leave the home studio where you've made pictures since the dawn of your career—more than fifteen years ago. You make a movie that means everything to you, but your power and your connections are so uncertain that your heartfelt work may never get released.

You try other media but end up with a succession of apparent failures. You've past fifty—not old, but with all these problems, is it possible your life and career will never recover?

Now, imagine you've kicked the pills and you've been given another chance to strut your stuff. It seems to work out pretty well, and while you're in postproduction you confidently begin work on your next project. Then, at that moment, the man who shepherded you through your chance at career renewal vanishes, the money he promised is gone, and both your projects are now in limbo.

Well, there's one man who doesn't have to imagine this scenario. This man actually lived everything I just described and more. And his name is Jerry Lewis.

Yes, I know—"they love him in France." But we love him in America, too. Because Jerry Lewis—win or lose—is always fascinating, always entertaining. At his best, he is a sublime clown, an innovative filmmaker, and a humanitarian of justifiable renown. At his worst, he is a pedantic, self-glorifying, desperate presence teetering on the edge for all to see. But in both these guises he is one of the most fascinating men on earth.

By 1978, Jerry Lewis, "the total filmmaker," had suffered a series of professional humiliations that would shake most mortals to the core. He had been addicted to the painkiller Percodan for more than a decade. He had not released a movie since 1970's *Which Way to the Front?*, which had hardly been a record breaker at the box office.

Jerry Lewis planned to make *That's Life*, a senior citizen's *Animal House*.

He had filmed a "serious" movie about a clown who entertained children on the way to the gas chambers in a World War II concentration camp, titled *The Day the Clown Cried*. The film, a French-Swedish coproduction, was edited by Jerry, then lost in litigation—never to be released.

His chain of family-oriented "Jerry Lewis Cinemas" collapsed into bankruptcy. He signed to star in the Broadway revival of the manic comedy *Hellzapoppin',* which closed before it ever reached Broadway. He was later reported as having come close to killing himself.

But for Jerry Lewis there would be yet another chance at redemption.

With the help of famed heart surgeon Dr. Michael DeBakey, Jerry put his addiction to Percodan behind him and learned to live with the back pain born of a thousand pratfalls. And he met a man, a Mr. Joseph Ford Proctor, who offered him the chance to be "the total filmmaker" all over again. Proctor lined up financing for a new Jerry Lewis film called *Hardly Working,* to be filmed in Florida during the first half of 1979.

Of course, Jerry never claimed his life problems had been the cause of his lengthy hiatus from films. To the contrary, he claimed he had been put off by the "decadence" that had set in during the porn-chic era of *Deep Throat* and societal disarray. And in fact, impresario Proctor sensed the time was right for another "Jerry" film when pictures like *Animal House* demonstrated that a market for his kind of comedy was once again ready to be tapped. But the fact remains that Jerry put his salary in escrow to demonstrate he was confident he could bring this baby in as promised.

Well, he did bring *Hardly Working* to a successful conclusion. A full-page ad in the March 8, 1979, *Hollywood Reporter* announced: "Jerry Lewis started filming Thursday, February 22nd, the same day George Washington started. He'll finish on Friday the 13th of April (that's his lucky day)." Beneath the text was a photo of Jerry as a bucktoothed Japanese chef and the credit: "Hardly Working: A Jerry Lewis Film."

Jerry was back—and seemingly with a vengeance!

On June 25, 1979, Army Archerd began his column in *Daily Variety:*

Good Morning: Jerry Lewis has once again created a studio-like setup—"a complete complex," he calls the 23 rooms he's expanded to at the Palm Air Country Club in Fort Lauderdale. Nine months ago, Jerry and Joe Proctor launched their first pic, Hardly Working, *down there. This Thursday, Jerry starts their second,* That's Life, *while cutting* Working *at night for Christmas release. He's also preparing their third,* Hardly Working Attacks Star Wars, *to start after his Labor Day telethon.*

On August 22, 1979, *Variety*'s Jack Zisk reported:

Jerry Lewis' return to Las Vegas last week for a Sahara engagement through the 29th, the financially troubled That's Life *film project has ceased operations at least until late September. Lengthy contractual negotiations with new investors blunted plans to resume shooting earlier this month. The film's crew, on standby for several weeks, has been told the project will resume no earlier than 9/24. Producer Igo Kantor estimates that efforts to hold the unit together in hopes of a quick settlement cost the project between $250,000 and $300,000.*

Financial "facilitator" Joseph Proctor had seemingly disappeared. Lewis and Igo Kantor found the money to complete postproduction on *Hardly Working*, but *That's Life* was never completed.

I can't say that the absence from America's film oeuvre of *Hardly Working Attacks Star Wars* is worth crying about. It may even be worth celebrating. But *That's Life* will be missed. It was described as a "senior citizen's *Animal House*" and was to star Academy Award winner Red Buttons, *Harold and Maude*'s Ruth Gordon, Yiddish theater veteran Molly Picon, and other notable oldsters. Jerry was not to star.

Though Jerry was younger than his leading actors, they were from his generation of show business. He had regained his directorial chops during the making of *Hardly Working*. Much of *Hardly Working* shows an uncertain hand, but his next "Jerry" movie, *Cracking Up,* features sequences of sheer Jerry brilliance. Shortly to make his mark as a serious actor in *The King of Comedy*, he was clearly at a moment of artistic rebirth, and it's a shame we'll never get to see this picture that played so strongly to his enthusiasms, experience, and strengths.

Jerry Lewis went on to other other lows (heart problems, divorce) and highs (the aforementioned *King of Comedy*, a new wife and baby). He has recently been touring the country in the musical *Damn Yankees*, which he previously played on Broadway. He was the highest-paid performer in the history of Broadway.

Unusually for Jerry, triumph emerged from this adversity. *Hardly Working* was a surprising box office success—not only abroad but in America as well. It gave Jerry a whole new career in movies. Yet *That's Life* was dead.

Timegate

In Timegate, *future humans routinely travel through time, so this is really a Jurassic park—filled with safer dinos and gated to protect its visitors.*

Some of the most satisfying films have come from the realm of the low budget. From the days of Val Lewton's RKO B unit (which produced classics like *The Curse of the Cat People*) to the modern era of independent film, money and cinematic quality have never gone hand in hand.

Many times, we look back at the slightly jerky stop-motion of older films and laugh at the primitivism that at the time seemed an astonishing imitation of life. The awesomely authentic effects of the original *Star Wars* were already rickety by the time of their augmentation in 1997's Special Edition. But almost no one would claim that the "new" *Star Wars* is a more effective movie than the original configuration, and 1933's *King Kong* still brings more terror and tears than the justifiably ignored period piece of the seventies.

During the aforementioned seventies, Jim Danforth was working on Universal's planned *King Kong* remake, which was to feature state-of-the-art stop-motion animation (the evolved version of the techniques used in the original *Kong*). One of the younger old-school guys, Danforth began his effects career in the early sixties with the movie *Atlantis, the Lost Continent.* He also worked on *7 Faces of Dr. Lao, When Dinosaurs Ruled the Earth,* and even *Flesh Gordon.*

The *Kong* on which Danforth was working was not the seventies *Kong* of which I spoke earlier. This was a rival production that never made it out of the starting gate. Both Universal and Dino De Laurentiis believed they had acquired rights to remake the property, and after much saber rattling the De Laurentiis-Paramount camp won, with Universal settling for a piece of the action.

Well, Danforth and his cronies, so proud of their handcrafted work, were incensed at the notion that the man-in-a-suit version of *Kong* had prevailed. Danforth and an associate from Universal threw around some ideas, and Danforth ended up pitching *Timegate,* which he would direct, as a low-budget showcase for the techniques he knew so well.

Timegate was in many respects a proto–*Jurassic Park.* In *Timegate,* a large corporation manages a "safe" prehistoric park, but the switch here is that the park is actually located in prehistoric times! In *Timegate,* future humans routinely travel through time, so this is *really* a Jurassic park—filled with safer dinos and gated to protect its visitors.

The principals in *Timegate* arrive at the park as part of a packaged dinosaur-hunting expedition. When dangerous prehistoric predators burst through the gates and damage the mechanism for surfing time, our heroes must make their way through the dangers of the reptile-laden past to find a distant outpost via which they can contact the people of their time and get help.

To cut costs, no scenes were to be set in the future. The film was to open with a small dinosaur peeling and eating eggs in the sand. Suddenly the *Timegate* opens in front of the creature and an eight-legged walking machine emerges carrying our adventurers and all their gear.

Eleven dinosaur species were lovingly resurrected for the film, which was to have contained 175 separate animation effects shots. Such giants of the field as Phil Tippett (later a dinosaur supervisor on *Jurassic Park*) and Ken Ralston (who worked on *Star Wars, Forrest Gump,* and *The Mask*) were part of the team, and the producers included Melvin (*Love at First Bite*) Simon and Milton (*Tales from the Crypt*) Subotsky. This was a team familiar with movies with budgets that ran from the thousands to the multimillions. They could do anything.

A facility to produce the models and effects was opened in July 1977. Publicity was avoided so that they could escape the unions' glare. A certified low-budget cast featuring the likes of June Lockhart, Barbara Bach, and Bo Svenson was being assembled, and Danforth's labor of love, his showcase of high-level classic effects, would feature dinosaurs, not just rampaging, but acting normally in their natural environment.

The planned effects evoked both the biologically primitive and the cinematically primitive. Even the old Commando Cody (*Rocket Man*) technique was to be utilized. Danforth even built a full-size "walking machine." He told an interviewer, "The walking machine was a concept I felt would be so strong on the screen, it justified the extra effect."

Unfortunately, expenses climbed and the budget grew from under a million to $2.4 million as Danforth kept rewriting his labor of love. "My fifth draft script," he said, "is a blueprint for a much more entertaining film than the first draft."

In August of 1978, American International Pictures joined the production, which scheduled an October start date. AIP demanded changes, and eventually Danforth could handle no more. He said that he wouldn't do any more rewrites, but he would direct the picture and continue to handle the effects.

He was subsequently locked out of his facility. There is some difference of opinion as to whether it was accidental or intentional, but Danforth resigned and the producers pulled the plug on the operation.

Danforth told a reporter, "We created a warehouse full of esoteric props and futuristic vehicles. We shot thousands of feet of second-unit background plates and high-speed miniatures." When the studio was closed, the props were thrown out for the taking.

Here's a team of guys who wanted to do something great. They wanted to do it on a budget. They wanted it to be so good that the budget grew. But they weren't making a big-budget movie. They were working with low-budget producers. Maybe there is *some* correlation between budget and quality. If only Danforth and his team had gone looking for *medium*-budget producers . . .

Vicky

Well, how would you like to practice some free love with me?

Vicky, based on the life of Victoria Woodhull, was written by James Toback, one of the finer screenwriters of the modern era. This is a screenplay about an American woman who promoted sexual freedom and women's rights, who traveled among the rich and famous, and who even ran for president—and she did all this during the 1800s. Toback's first produced screenplay was *The Gambler,* and he both wrote and directed the films *Love and Money* and *The Pick-up Artist.* He also wrote *Bugsy* for Warren Beatty and Barry Levinson. *Vicky* has long been close to Toback's heart, and though it was originally slated for production during the 1970s, he has returned to it and revised it many times, as recently as 1996.

George Barrie, owner of the fragrance company Fabergé, was a fan of *The Gambler* and had intended to produce *Vicky* back in the seventies. Faye Dunaway was to have starred, and George Cukor (who had directed Katherine Hepburn in films like *Adam's Rib*) was to have directed. Toback had originally wanted to direct it himself, but, believe it or not, the then-retired Cary Grant (who was on the Fabergé board of directors) was considering doing the film and Cukor was a director with whom he felt comfortable.

Writer-director James Toback's film on the life of Victoria Woodhull would never see the light of the silver screen.

Fortunately, Toback felt comfortable with Cukor as well and they prepared the film together. Cukor was in the latter part of his career but by no means finished. Completely involved with the writer in developing the film, Cukor had Toback rewrite the screenplay again and again. Cukor would have Toback read scenes to him over and over until Toback noticed something was needed (usually something Cukor had already recognized as necessary). The results of this attention to detail are impressive.

Toback has long been a student of history, reading the letters of historical figures and studying their times. As a result, his characters in *Vicky* do not sound entirely contemporary, yet their speech is not the theatrical faux-period dialogue we are accustomed to hearing in such pieces. Rather, the characters speak a natural-sounding dialect that just happens to be (slightly) different from our own.

Here is a sample exchange from a sequence that begins with soapbox orator Bennie Tucker waxing enthusiastic on a New York street:

Bennie: I am an anarchist, an atheist. I am not ashamed. I submit freely to who I am—an internationalist, a free trader, a suffragist, a champion of the eight-hour day, an enemy of marriage and a believer in complete sexual freedom. In short, I am a man of my age!

There are some cheers and some boos. One man calls out: "You're not a man, you're a baby!" Bennie turns on him.

Bennie: I am a good deal older than I look, I assure you. And besides, I've had a great deal of experience for my age.

There is again a loud reaction.

Vicky: Let's take him home with us.

She looks at Tennessee, who laughs, then at James, who understands, accepts it. Vicky approaches Bennie and speaks to him privately.

Vicky: Do you just preach all those wonderful ways of being or do you practice them as well?

Bennie: I practice them—of course!

Vicky: Of course. Well, how would you like to practice some free love with me?

Bennie: (flustered)
Yes . . . Well, I'm certain that—

Vicky: Are you a virgin?

Bennie: A virgin! I've been everywhere. I've done everything.

Vicky: Prove it. Show me.

The characters' syntax is slightly more formal than what we favor today, but they are direct and clear—real people. And what people they are. We think that a liberal mind-set is the peculiar hallmark of our advanced place in time, but these characters—based on authentic historical characters—demonstrate that the past was not a serene garden of biblical thought. It was populated by individuals whose intellect and impulses were every bit the equal of our own.

Unfortunately, the choice of director Cukor, so fortuitous in terms of luring Cary Grant, turned out to be less than fortuitous when it came to lining up financing. Cukor's big-budget *The Blue Bird* came out while *Vicky* was in development, and its failure soured the industry on the old man. (For the moment. He did direct again.)

Toback managed to dredge personal triumph from adversity by guilting George Barrie into financing *Fingers,* his directorial debut. But *Vicky* languished on the shelf until Warren Beatty took up its cause in the midnineties. Beatty took it to Laura Ziskin of Fox 2000 Films, who—in her own words—"wimped out" and rejected it.

And she was considered the film's best chance of getting made.

Toback feels that the Hollywood studio heads are behind even the mall goers of America's middle class in their understanding of what will work on the screen. He believes ordinary Americans would embrace *Vicky,* with its large canvas of nineteenth-century events and people like Cornelius Vanderbilt, Frederick Douglass, and Henry Ward Beecher.

Toback is right. This is Academy Award–winning material.

It's ironic that one of the compelling features of *Vicky* is that it's a film about a woman who's ahead of her time. The screenplay is a historically founded roundelay of sex, ambition, fraud, politics, and humanity. But Vicky comes across ahead of her time because she feels so much like certain women of our own time. Other important proto-feminists like Susan B. Anthony were also a part of Vicky's landscape (and also appear in the film). And the abandon of the 1920s was still to come between Vicky's time and our own. We of the present are not the end-all of human development. We are not very different from our forebears at all.

Indeed, if modern-day film executives are to be believed, Americans of the past were more advanced than Americans of today. Because in the world of *Vicky* people of the 1870s lived and thought at a level of sophistication deemed inappropriate for audiences today. And in the 1970s it was possible to get such a movie made.

But not in the cinematically devolved future that is today.

*When McClory approached him about affiliating
with his rival Bond property, Connery immediately
attached himself to the project, but not as an actor—
as a writer!*

Most everybody knows that Ian Fleming created James Bond. But
what does creation mean when it comes to a pop cultural figure
who has passed through so many hands? Wasn't the James Bond of
popular conception as much created by Sean Connery's performance
as by some writer's toil? Didn't Albert R. Broccoli and Harry Saltz-
man's production touch "create" the cinematic environment that au-
thenticates James Bond? If you put a guy in a tux and shoot him
through a gun barrel while John Barry's music plays in the background, isn't he James Bond?

After all, *Casino Royale* is nominally a James Bond movie and stars
David Niven, who Ian Fleming considered appropriate for the role,
but is it really Bond? And doesn't *Never Say Never Again* seem somehow unofficial because it doesn't have the production underpinnings
of a "legitimate" entry?

Still, *Never Say Never Again* does have the only other element that
can make a Bond movie "legitimate" in the public mind. It stars Sean
Connery, who somehow is Bond in a way Roger Moore, George

Lazenby, and the other successors will never be, even as they star in "Bond movies" that are unassailably "real."

There are two legitimizing authorities when it comes to James Bond movies:

The Brocolli/UA production camp makes "real" James Bond movies.

Sean Connery is the "real" James Bond.

Likewise, there have been two strains of James Bond ownership—the aforementioned Albert R. Broccoli/MGM/UA strain and the Kevin McClory strain, less well-known but still quite potent.

You see, before Bond was ever presented on the big screen author Ian Fleming teamed with film-

Sean Connery's planned return to the James Bond franchise in *Warhead* was simply not meant to be.

maker McClory to develop a James Bond movie. Their original screenplay (written with Jack Whittingham) was called *Thunderball,* and when Fleming shortly turned it into a novel without giving his collaborators credit a legal process began that created two separate holders of the film rights to 007.

McClory could easily have ended up like the guys who held rights to *Casino Royale*—as an outsider, a guy who just wasn't "authentic." However, Fleming and the official team had utilized concepts and characters that were created by the McClory team before legal questions of ownership were settled. In addition, they had invited McClory to partner with them on the production of *Thunderball.* The effects were as follows:

1. Producing Thunderball gave McClory the credibility that came with being the producer of an official entry in the Bond series.

2. When the legal issues were settled, McClory ended up owning characters and concepts that had already been utilized in the official series—things he could use to make his films seem official, things the "official" guys could no longer use at all.

Now, McClory had agreed not to produce additional Bond films until 10 years after *Thunderball*. Fortunately, in the mid-1970s James Bond was as viable a commodity as ever. So, as soon as he was able, McClory began making plans to produce another Bond film of his own. It was to be based on elements of the Bond property that he owned—not a remake of *Thunderball*, but a picture using many of the characters and situations that had been developed during *Thunderball*'s creation.

The saga of *Thunderball*'s creation had taken place between 1959 and 1961. McClory's 1958 film, *The Boy and the Bridge*, attracted Ian Fleming's attention, and the two agreed to collaborate on a Bond film that McClory intended to direct. The first tangible development of the story accompanied a memo sent by their associate Ernest Cuneo on May 28, 1959. The memo read:

> *Enclosed was written at-night, mere improvisation hence far from author's pride, possible author's mortification. Haven't even re-read it.*
>
> *. . . Ernest Cuneo*

The memo detailed a quickly abandoned star-studded plot reminiscent of Mike Todd's *Around the World in 80 Days*. (McClory had worked for Todd.) It set off a round of story development that resulted in the collection of characters and concepts ultimately owned by McClory. Among the characters was villain Ernst Stavro Blofeld, and among the concepts was SPECTRE, the evil organization so prominent in early "official" Bonds. (In fact, there is considerable testimony supporting the claim that McClory created SPECTRE, an important element of the Bond mythos.)

In the mid-seventies, armed with the notes, script drafts, and treatments developed during the *Thunderball* sessions, McClory set about developing *Warhead* (aka *James Bond of the Secret Service*). During this era, Sean Connery's relationship with the "official" Bond producers was not a fond one—he felt he had never been paid what he was worth. When McClory approached Connery about affiliating with his rival Bond property, he immediately attached himself to the project, but not as an actor—as a writer! He didn't feel like playing Bond again, but he knew his name on the project would draw attention and antagonize Broccoli. (Apparently, many of the funny one-liners in the *Warhead* script originated with Connery.)

The 1978 *Warhead* project was in many ways an attempt to do an authentic Bond movie at a time when the UA series had strayed from some of its stylistic origins. Connery had so much fun collaborating on the script that he agreed to star in the film. Orson Welles was to bring grandiosity and star power to the project as Blofeld. Bond would even drive his trademark Aston Martin, which by now was missing from the "official" series.

Blofeld was to live underwater in something called the Aquapolis. Sharks were to have infested the New York sewer system and gotten into the New York Stock Exchange. Sean Connery elaborated on the plot:

> We had all sorts of exotic events. You know those airplanes that were disappearing over the Bermuda triangle? We had SPECTRE doing that. There was this fantastic fleet of planes underneath the sea—a whole world of stuff that had been brought down. They were going to attack the financial nerve center of the United States by going in through the sewers of New York—which you can do—right

into Wall Street. They'd have mechanical sharks in the bay and take over the Statue of Liberty, which is quite easy, and have the main troops on Ellis Island. That sort of thing.

Unfortunately, the legal and financial muscle of United Artists and Albert "Cubby" Broccoli's organization was employed to squash their onetime collaborator. The UA camp even employed Fleming's estate to assist them. The legal threats from the "official" camp frightened potential investors, and *Warhead* was never made.

Because of McClory's claims on Blofeld and SPECTRE, the "official" films haven't (overtly) used either in more than twenty years. Likewise, nobody on the Broccoli side was willing to question McClory's right to flat-out re-create *Thunderball*. So, McClory and Connery finally took a shot at Broccoli via the halfhearted 1983 *Thunderball* remake, *Never Say Never Again*.

Sadly, the dream of doing a new alternate "real" Bond (as opposed to a remake) long seemed dead. But recently Sony acquired McClory's rights, and now his properties have financial and legal strength equal to those of the "official" camp. While McClory's claims to the properties were once quite strong, various maneuverings may, in fact, have weakened them. But Sony seems confident, to the point of claiming the UA camp (now controlled by MGM) actually owes them a percentage of the profits from the entire series because McClory properties served as its underpinning.

Whichever way it turns out, it is certain that we will never see Orson Welles's Blofeld and that Connery will never be under fifty (or sixty) again. So the 1978 notion of *Warhead* is forever lost to us.

Won't Fade Out

... Won't Fade Out *is about a group of venerable actors on a European tour to promote a* That's Entertainment*–style film celebrating their classic performances.*

In recent years trailers have become more like condensed versions of the films they promote. They explain everything that happens in a film, including its resolution. Movie studios believe it's so hard to get someone into the theater that they must reveal as much as possible in order to let the audience know the movie in question is for *them*.

Why would a potential audience member go to a movie if he or she already knew how it was going to end? Perhaps to see it fleshed out or maybe, in effect, to see it *again*. We've been trained not to expect surprises from our various forms of theater. Critics reveal a film's every detail by opening day, so the only way to see a film without foreknowledge is by being a critic. And just as audiences know everything about a film going in, it's gotten to the point where Hollywood executives want to know everything before a film is even produced. Executives want new movies to be like movies that have been made before, and film artists are expected to make films in keeping with audience expectations.

Of course, audiences prove every day that they want more than what Hollywood offers, hence the rise of so-called independent films. But Hollywood executives are generally not artists, and their careers are about power rather than product. They fear creativity because it's unpredictable, so they cling to whatever formulas they can.

The rise to prominence of screenwriting gurus is an example of this phenomenon. Aspiring screenwriters are told what kinds of characters they need, when "conflict" must commence, and what is supposed to happen on specific pages of their work. It's an easy way to produce something recognizable as a screenplay to the executives who follow the very same gurus. Fearing for their jobs and without creativity, film executives cling to these rules as if they were life preservers. That's why we get cookie-cutter movies from Hollywood.

Andrew J. Lederer found himself heading toward a brick wall of these rules when he wrote *Won't Fade Out,* a loving but cynical look at the Hollywood of old trapped in the world of the present. Designed to showcase every remaining star from Hollywood's golden age, *Won't Fade Out* is about a group of venerable actors on a European tour to promote a *That's Entertainment*–style film celebrating their classic performances.

Starting in comedy as a teenager, Lederer had moved on to acting roles in movies and television before moving behind the scenes when a film he acted in was deemed unreleasable. The director asked Lederer to collaborate on a restructuring of the film that included additional shooting and the recording of a narration that Lederer wrote. Lederer even co-crafted the ad campaign for the film, which was called *Out of Control.*

Unfortunately, even the "releasable" version of *Out of Control* was too quirky, and a fearful New World Pictures refused to screen it for reviewers. The picture then received a rave review from the *LA Times,* but a profitable opening weekend had been lost, as the review didn't appear until Monday. Despite this crash course in Hollywood timidity, Lederer—his background in stand-up—was essentially a storyteller, and he turned his attention toward screenwriting.

He sent two scripts to producer Fred Weintraub, who told him,

"You're a writer," which emboldened Lederer to try something more ambitious than the genre films he had been crafting. He wrote a story in which the stress of a publicity tour rips a group of elderly actors apart. Old wounds are reopened, illnesses are inflamed, and interpersonal dynamics that have spanned the decades come back into play.

The old troupers are treated like meat by their handlers. One character is a stroke victim, another tethered to a wheelchair and an oxygen tank, yet another two steps from crumbling to dust. Eventually, a debt-ridden former star, worth more dead than alive, decides to exploit his weary comrades. He needs insurance money to protect his family, but if he commits suicide, the company won't pay. So he gathers his associates in a hotel ballroom and demogogically implores them to go out the way they lived—in a blaze of glory, as *stars!* He convinces them to commit mass suicide but make it look like an accident. A boiler would be set to explode in that very ballroom. The last stars of Hollywood's golden age would vanish instantly, shockingly, and completely. The last thing they did, both individually and as a generation, would be front-page news, and then they would be gone. They would not fade out.

Unfortunately, when the gang gathers to enact the plan, only one person is missing—its instigator. Racing toward the hotel, desperately trying to make it in time, he collapses to the sidewalk with a heart attack.

Unaware of his fate, the other stars begin to feel they've been had. They clamor to escape, but before they can get out, the ballroom explodes. Unexpectedly, however, the mastermind of the plan survives his cardiac incident and becomes the last remaining star from Hollywood's golden age. As he is then much in demand, his financial problems have been entirely eliminated.

On a talk show, he speaks sadly of his cronies' "accident" as we . . . fade out.

The script is sad, unsettling . . . and very funny. A director of comedies for Showtime told Andrew it reminded him of the classic *It's a*

Mad, Mad, Mad, Mad World and said audiences would be excited by the prospect of spotting all the old players. There were parts for Frank Sinatra, Burt Lancaster, Bette Davis, James Stewart, Ralph Bellamy, Roy Rogers, Ginger Rogers, the surviving Little Rascals, Lillian Gish— just about every former star who was alive at the time.

Paramount Pictures considered the script after one of its vice presidents struck up an acquaintanceship with Lederer at an LA comedy club. However, it was ultimately rejected because of that old bugaboo—expectations. The Paramount executive was disappointed because he expected the script to simply be funny while it was actually rather a sad dark comedy. Lederer had never promised it would be "funny." But he was a comedian, and from comedians Hollywood wants flat-out comedies.

The fortunate few who have read the script have marveled at its heart and dimensionality as well as the blackness of its comedy. While the script was in play, there was talk of having John Frankenheimer direct it in the black comic style of his *The Comedian*. There are actors like Gloria Stuart who could star in the picture today, but so many of the awesome greats for whom it was designed have now faded away. (Of course, there will be new generations of oldsters who could play it as their generation's swan song.) Like so many others, the script remains unmade and, though great, may itself be forced to simply fade out.

50 More of the Greatest Movies Never Made

have a confession to make. The original title of this book was *The 100 Greatest Movies Never Made*. Sounds cool, huh? It rolls off the tongue and fits well with all those other "100" list types of books. (Personally, I despise those meaningless "100 Whatever List" types of books. They are the cause of more worthless arguments amongst cinephiles.)

By no means is the book you are reading incomplete; I simply had to make some tough (in some cases, painful) choices about what to include and what to save for a potential sequel.

The films I had to leave on the "cutting room floor," so to speak, would make an excellent follow-up. It kills me to not be able to tell you in detail about David Lynch's unmade epic, *Ronnie Rocket*. The bizarre script featured a diminutive alien from Mars (to be played by the midget from *Twin Peaks* in the starring role) and his unbelievable exploits on Earth. The poetic script for *Ronnie Rocket* by Lynch and writing partner Mark Frost is available to read; however, the amazing visuals are, unfortunately, forever tucked away in Lynch's mind and will never be committed to celluloid. (Luckily, the script is being turned into a graphic novel, a comic book to be published out of Japan.)

There is an amazing script for *The Watchman* written by *Batman* movie scribe Sam Hamm. The comic book on which the script is based was written by legendary comic author Alan Moore and illustrated by Dave Gibbons. The 12-issue graphic novel series, also available as a collected volume, poses the questions: What if costumed vigilantes really existed? How would society respond to them? These costumed heroes are soon legislated out of existence by corrupt politicians until a plot develops that threatens the world. This comic book is as cinematic as it is epic. It screams, "Make me into a movie!" The project was actually developed by none other than Terry (*12 Monkeys, Brazil*) Gilliam for him to direct. (That leads me to another Terry Gilliam film, *The Defective Detective,* another visually arresting comic book–like tale, also gathering dust as a script on a shelf.)

Another wonderful film that never saw the light of a movie projector is *Flamingoes Forever*, the sequel to John Waters's now-classic *Pink Flamingoes*. The film was to feature Divine riding a giant turd (yes, a turd!) like a magic carpet in all her glory. The film was not to be, as Divine's tragic death halted Waters's plans to make the film.

There are so many others; imagine if you will . . .

Noriega, written and directed by Oliver Stone, to star James Woods in the starring role as the fanatical dictator . . .

The Simpsons Movie, based on the popular Fox cartoon show, which has been talked about for years . . .

A Fatty Arbuckle bio-pic about the tragic life of the silent film star that was written by David Mamet and was to star Chris Farley before his untimely death . . .

A Velvet Glove Cast in Iron, based on the indie comic book by Daniel Clowes, which has the cinematic feel of a great unmade art film . . .

Little Demons, a bizarre musical by Oingo Boingo lead singer and movie soundtrack king Danny Elfman, who recorded the soundtrack and wrote the songs but never made the film . . .

The hilarious parody of the Indiana Jones films called *Cleveland*

Smith Bounty Hunter, bragging brilliant script by Scott Spiegel and Josh Becker, to be produced by Sam Raimi. The filmmakers did make a 10-minute short starring Bruce Campbell but failed to secure funding . . .

A film version of the book A *Confederacy of Dunces*, which many have tried to bring to the screen, including Harold Ramis and John Waters, though no one has succeeded . . .

The film of *Geek Love*, another great book about freaks that remains unmade . . .

The Mitchell Brothers, a tragic bio-pic about the owners of San Francisco's famous adult theater, brothers involved in a shocking murder . . .

Strawberry Fields Forever, planned to be a semisequel to the Beatles' *Yellow Submarine*. The movie was going to be the first all computer-generated film before Disney's *Toy Story* and was to have featured Beatles music. The filmmakers even went so far as to produce 10 minutes of test footage, which has never been seen . . .

A failed James Dean bio-pic with an incredible script by Israel Horovitz and Michael Mann, the best Dean bio-pic ever written, yet never produced . . .

Xenogenesis, a great unmade James Cameron sci-fi epic for which he shot test footage but, unfortunately, could not raise the financing . . .

Plastic Man, the story of a superhero who can stretch his body, to have starred Pee-wee Herman actor Paul Reubens and to have been directed by Tim Burton . . .

Up against It, a live-action film to have starred the Beatles written by Joe Orton . . .

And so many more. Too many to count. But enough perhaps for another book. . . .

If you truly would like to read about 50 More of the Greatest Movies Never Made, buy more copies of this book. Better yet, barrage St. Martin's Press with requests. Their web site is www.stmartins.com.

If you know of some great unfinished films that should appear in a potential sequel, drop me a line at: Chris Gore, c/o *Film Threat*, 5042 Wilshire Blvd. Suite 150, Los Angeles, CA 90036.

About the Author

CHRIS GORE founded *Film Threat* as a college fanzine in Detroit in 1985. As the fanzine evolved into a respected national magazine, he relocated to Los Angeles in 1989. The magazine became the leading source for information about the growing explosion of independent films.

Chris Gore has been called everything from " . . . the Gen-X Leonard Maltin" to the "pit bull of journalism." He is the publisher of *Film Threat* (www.filmthreat.com) and is currently developing a pilot for a TV show for American Movie Classics.

In addition, he has written screenplays, none of which have been produced. Yet.